THE STORY WRITER

THE STORY WRITER

By Edith Ronald Mirrielees

ASSOCIATE PROFESSOR OF ENGLISH
AT STANFORD UNIVERSITY

THE WRITER, INC.,
8 ARLINGTON STREET
BOSTON, MASS.

Thanks for help in the composition of this book are due to my colleagues on the staff of the Bread Loaf Writers' Conference; to many students, both at Bread Loaf and at Stanford University; and especially to Mr. Theodore Morrison, Director of the Conference, to Mrs. Helen Everitt, at whose suggestion the book was begun, and to Mrs. May Hurlburt Smith, whose emendations are included in many of the chapters.

Contents

I

TO USE A BOOK

. . . as for the amateur, his difficulty is that his work, once on the page, hardens as cement hardens and can no more be changed. When he has learned to change it, to consider it in this light, to consider it in that, to hold the subject warm in his affections at the same time that his mind appraises the form — when that time comes, he is no longer an amateur.

Suggested Reading

HAWTHORNE, NATHANIEL. *American Notebooks*. New Haven, Yale University Press

MONTAGUE, C. C. *A Writer's Notes on His Trade*. London, Chatto and Windus

CONRAD, JOSEPH. *A Personal Record*. Garden City, Doubleday, Doran

CANFIELD, DOROTHY. *Raw Material*. New York, Harcourt, Brace

MAUGHAM, SOMERSET. *The Summing Up*. Garden City, Doubleday, Doran

KIPLING, RUDYARD. *Something of Myself*. Garden City, Doubleday, Doran

WELLS, H. G. *An Experiment in Autobiography*. New York, Macmillan

CHEKHOV, ANTON. *The Notebook of Anton Chekhov*. New York, The Viking Press

DE LA MARE, WALTER. *Poetry in Prose*. New York, Oxford University Press

QUILLER-COUCH, SIR ARTHUR. *On the Art of Writing*. New York, G. P. Putnam's Sons

ANDERSON, SHERWOOD. *The Modern Writer*. San Francisco, The Lantern Press

To Use a Book

I

NEARLY every person who opens this book will do so for two reasons. He will be in search of means for the general improvement of his writing; and he will also be trying to find out how to subdue a particular refractory story. The greater part of either struggle has to be carried on unaided, but there are certain limited helps which, with sufficient effort on the reader's part, can be made to come from a book. The purpose of this opening chapter, then, is to point out what a book can and what it cannot do, and how this especial book is intended to be used.

First, for the impossibilities: Between the arrival of the idea or feeling which is to grow into a story and the deposit in mind or on paper of its first rough draft, neither book nor any other thing can profitably intervene between the writer and his subject. Those well-meant critical aids — "Wouldn't it be more interesting if you put a woman instead of a man in the life-boat?" "I've thought of something

that could happen to him right after he gets home"
— may, once in a hundred times, improve one patch-
work story, but they invariably weaken the writer
of it. So usually do the more formal assistances
which urge the beginner towards plot outlines and
diagrams and other Procrustean stretchings. Writing
is necessarily a lonely business. Only by repeated,
unaided struggles to shape his material to his
own purpose does a beginner grow into a writer.
There are some helps towards general improvement which can be given. There are many specific
helps in the work of revision. But help in the initial
conception of a story there is none. That is the
writer's own affair.

II

It being granted, then, that the thinking out of
any one story is the work of the writer and of the
writer only, what help looking towards the improvement of all his stories can a book offer? Aided
by sufficient intelligent application on his own part,
it can offer four kinds:

It can increase the amount of his meditating about
writing — about what stories try to do and the ways
open to them for doing it.

It can strengthen his recognition of cause and
effect.

It can keep him awake to the general applications of specific happenings.

It can improve his use of words, the only blocks he has to build with.

To extract these helps, however, any reader has to make large contributions of his own. Passive reading arrives nowhere.

In a reading which looks towards general improvement, probably the best way to deal with this book is to read first the chapter, *The Substance of the Story,* reading it through from beginning to end, marking passages likely to be useful to you, blocking off those inapplicable to your kind of writing, putting question marks beside the ones you disagree with or do not understand.

This reading is a first step advisable for all readers alike. Ordinarily, but not invariably, the second step is to read several of the stories listed at the beginning of the chapter, reading not more than one in a day or in several days but rereading that one often enough to make yourself familiar with it. You are familiar with it when both its incidents and the thread which holds those incidents together are clear in your mind; when you see why the writer has chosen to open his story at a particular point and to tell it in a particular way; when you have read passages from it aloud often enough to get and relish their tune, the ring of their sentences. Not every story among those recommended is of equal excellence. Not every one is for every reader. Rejection of those which are below or above your present level of appreciation is a not unimportant part of the business of learning.

Stories listed at the beginning of each chapter are, as a rule, stories strictly contemporary. They are to be found in volumes still in print or in the files of magazines accessible in almost any public or college library. Both for the aid of readers whose library opportunities are few and for the sake of presenting a view of short fiction other than the contemporary, a set of older stories is placed at the end of the book. Even when the contemporary stories are at hand, it can do no reader harm to discover through his own rereading what the charm is which has kept alive "The Open Boat" and "Posson Jone'" and "The Love Letters of Smith", along with the more widely known tales of Irving and Hawthorne and Poe.

When three or four of the listed stories, either old or new, are clearly in mind, go back to *Substance* and reread it, changing your markings, jotting in your additions or reservations in the light of what the study of those three or four has taught you.

Proceed then to the other chapters in the same

slow fashion, reading the chapter, familiarizing yourself with some of the stories given, rereading the chapter, but, with each one, broadening the base of your consideration. A story listed under *Time* is as useful for study of substance as though it had been given the other listing. A story listed under *Substance* — for example "The Gentleman from San Francisco" — might as readily appear under *Character* or *Time*. If you are working in a class or with a group, your discoveries and decisions will, of course, be continually measured against those of the other members. Frequently the measurement will be markedly to your advantage, but no measure and no outside suggestion can replace the steady individual effort required at every step in writing.

III

While, through reading and study, you are trying for general improvement, you are also presumably at work upon a story of your own. For that individual story too, it is necessary to remember that not all of any set of suggestions made in any book is applicable to every reader. The practice you have had, the degree to which you have profited by practice, your native ability, the conditions under which you are working — all these you need to take account of for yourself. Having taken account, you then modify examples and procedures to fit your own needs.

Let us say that you have, to date, written four stories, each the product of twelve or fourteen hours of labor; that you are now at work on a fifth; and that the four already written have been sent and re-sent to editors, all of them being, in your own eyes, worthy of publication. You are, that is, the very worst variety of amateur, the one who not only knows not but knows not that he knows not. It is from this depth and by means of your fifth story that a book is to assist you.

Its first assistance is to cause you to remind yourself that twelve or fourteen hours of effort does not, ordinarily, make a story. It makes only the skeleton of a story, sometimes a mere rib. Expectation of quick results is the bane of amateur writing. The process of learning to write can be hurried only in direct ratio to the amount of your genius and the time at your disposal. Unless you are prepared to put on your earlier stories as much time, as many hours of intelligent effort, as go into the carrying and passing of a course in law or medicine, and unless you are ready, too, to admit that one story is to a would-be writer only what one course is to a prospective doctor or lawyer, then probably you would be wise to tear the fifth story up and turn what persistence you have in another direction. If, however, you do have the persistence for keeping on, you sit down with the completed draft of your story in front of you — that draft which, without outside warning, you would have been shipping off to editors. It is already as nearly perfect as you know how to make it. If it is to be better, it has to be through your learning to see and remedy its imperfections.

Probably you have already been asking yourself along the way what your story is about and how its incidents bring out its substance. Unless, though, these questions have been asked and many times answered before the written draft is finished, they are not the ones with which to begin now. If you have thought a story through without knowing what it is about, you will discover, if at all, only by way of the rearranging and chipping and rubbing which go to make up revision. Or it may be you are one of the writers who need never consciously consider the foundation ideas of their stories. At any rate, begin with questions more limited.

Reread your opening pages with your attention fixed on one matter only — say, the placing of them in time. Do they show the time at which the telling begins? Why does it begin at that point? What have the paragraphs preceding the first time break con-

tributed to the story? When you have answered
these questions to your satisfaction or partial satisfaction, read slowly through the whole story, marking, in mind or margin, the transitions by which
it moves from one point in time to another, noting
any omissions of considerable blocks of time and
accounting to yourself both for the omissions and
for the way in which you have made readers aware
of them. That done, lay the story aside for a few
days. Within these days, read the chapter on *Time,*
marking, blocking and questioning as in *Substance.*
Select a story from the list given at the beginning
of the chapter and read it, bringing the passages
just marked to bear on it. Does it uphold them? Or
can you — remember we are making you the worst
of amateurs — see simply no connection at all? If
this is true, choose another story from the list and
apply to it one of the simpler suggestions from the
text, perhaps ". . . the time of a happening in the
story and the intervals between happening and happening must be kept clear." With this new story,
keep your mind fixed only on its time changes and
the way the writer has marked them. Turn back
to your own story and consider it with this sentence
and this sentence only in mind, blocking in, however awkwardly, the alterations required. This being
done, try another passage from the text against

one of the listed stories — say, the passage dealing with general and special causes. Do not try it against your own story until you are entirely sure you understand what general and special causes are. One way to be sure is to write out for yourself what are the general causes, what the special one, in the story you have just read.

There will be some things in any story you are writing about which you are already sure. You know, for example, that the story must be told from a given point of observation; it will not be your story, the story you want, unless it is so told. Those certainties are not to be tampered with. No matter what advice, spoken or written, points in another direction, your story has to stay yours. It should change only as you come to feel it ought to change. Even though your feeling is wrong, it is better for your development as a writer to be wrong than to be supine.

But in matters where you do not have a fixed conviction, bring story against chapter in the fashion just suggested, allowing yourself continual opportunity for trying your impressions on stories not your own. When story number five has come again to what seems to you perfection, or when your mind has become so confused about it that you can no longer make decisions, put five away to cool, working on four or six until five is ready for further improvement.

All of this labor, this analysis of other people's stories and of your own, this revising and re-revising and putting away to cool, means staying a long time with one story. Most stories that are to be stories need to be stayed with a long time. Especially most beginners' stories do. Whether that staying is to be done before the first word comes to paper or whether it is to be done after the rough draft is set down is a matter of a writer's individual habit, but somewhere time has to be spent. Flitter-mindedness — a new idea every week and interest in the old one dead and gone — is one of the handicaps which keep a would-be writer would-be and no more to the end of his writing days.

II

THE SUBSTANCE OF THE STORY

To understand social reality, one must be inside it, participate in its movements and its struggles.
— IGNAZIO SILONE, *Bread and Wine*

Suggested Reading

BENÉT, STEPHEN VINCENT. "Everybody Was Very Nice." *Thirteen O'Clock*. New York, Farrar and Rinehart

BENSON, STELLA. "Protection." *Harper's Magazine*, December, 1933

BUNIN, IVAN A. "The Gentleman from San Francisco." *The Gentleman from San Francisco and Other Stories*. New York, A. A. Knopf

CONRAD, JOSEPH. *The Shadow Line*. Garden City, Doubleday, Doran

DAVIS, ELMER. "Bride of Quietness." *Harper's Magazine*, September, 1926

DAY, CLARENCE. "The Rabbits Conquer Fear." *The New Yorker*, December 9, 1933

HEYWARD, DU BOSE. *The Half-Pint Flask*. New York, Farrar and Rinehart

EDMONDS, WALTER D. "Young Ames." *Saturday Evening Post*, March 19, 1935

FROST, FRANCES. "Piano Prelude." *Yale Review*, Winter, 1938

NEWMAN, FRANCES. "Rachel Mourning for Her Children." *American Mercury*, May, 1924

PARKER, DOROTHY. "Horsie." *After Such Pleasures*. New York, The Viking Press

PORTOR, LAURA SPENCER. "The Mouse." *Harper's Magazine*, November, 1928

RINEHART, MARY ROBERTS. "Lightning Never Strikes Twice." *Saturday Evening Post*, June 6, 1936

SAROYAN, WILLIAM. "Seventy Thousand Assyrians." *The Daring Young Man on the Flying Trapeze*. New York, Random House

WELLS, H. G. "The Country of the Blind." *The Country of the Blind and Other Stories*. London, Thomas Nelson and Sons

The Substance of the Story

I

"THERE is a limit to the profitable elaboration of the obvious."

The originator of the above quotation is unknown, but internal evidence points towards his having been the reader for some large-size, fiction-publishing weekly.

In one sense it is true, as asserted in nearly every discussion of fiction writing, that there is no such thing as stale material, that any human situation lends itself to fictive treatment. None the less, stories fail for staleness, for lack of substance, for elaboration of the obvious, even oftener than from the writer's not knowing how to bring out what he intends to say. One of the questions a beginner at writing is called upon to put to himself when his first draft is finished, and often even earlier than that, is "What is my story about?" If he arrives at the answer, "It is about Herbert's marrying Sylvia", then the question should be put again and with a stronger emphasis, "But what is it *about*?" A story is almost never only about the marriage of Herbert to Sylvia any more than it is only about a shipwreck or a battle or a death or the finding of a gold mine. Now and then a writer writes a really good story without himself realizing, at any stage in the writing, what that story is, but such an adventure is rare. In the thinking out of most stories, the thing the story is about, as apart from merely what happens in it, is of the utmost importance.

For a story is not the sum of its happenings.

That statement deserves the dignity of a paragraph to itself. With the fewest exceptions a story is never merely a problem in addition, occurrence added to occurrence till the telling is done. To see why it is not it is necessary only to look at daily living, the source material for all fiction.

For any being living it, life is more than the march of successive happenings. A bookkeeper goes to his office, bends over his books, lunches at a neighboring drug store, goes home to listen to his radio, to fret at his wife. Does this make up life for him? His life is no such flat and open page. What does make it up is the many-colored thread of feeling which runs through the happenings and gives cohesion to them. Dread of poverty, anxiety about his family's future, an artist's pleasure in his own exactness, a dream of advancement to come, an odd-hours hobby, a dogged loyalty — any or all of these may be components of the thread. And each important component is both a part of the bookkeeper's inner life and also some small fraction of the inner life of any reader who can comprehend or be interested in him. The incidents of the two lives may have no point in common, but except superficially it is not the incidents for which the reader reads. It is for the man concerned in them. Incident piled on incident no more makes life than brick piled on brick makes a house. Neither does incident piled on incident make a story. Something beyond the incidents is essential to turn a set of happenings into fiction.

One chief importance of grasping the difference between piled happenings and stories is that, really grasped, the understanding of that difference regulates a beginner's writing habits. For since a story is other than the sum of its incidents, the reiterated truths about the uses of practice are half-truths only. Practice is indeed essential to writing, as essential as to violin playing. But practice alone accomplishes nothing. It may go on day in and day out, has gone on so through years, with a grinding, unflagging, heartbreaking persistence, and yet has produced no marked improvement in output. A writer's belief that persistence is all and is bound to be rewarded has no more foundation than that other belief, common to those who do not write, that authorship arrives by unaided inspiration. For fiction, if it is to be readable, comes not out of one thing but out of two — first, out of having something to say; and second, out of an unending diligence in trying to say it. Most of the chapters in this book deal with ways of saying it. This one deals with the even more important matter of having something to say.

To have that something, it is by no means necessary to have undergone bizarre experiences. Not many people have had unusual adventures; all people, without exception, have had adventures enough to provide for lifetimes of story writing. Everybody has been a child, has grown up, fallen in love, fallen out of love. Everybody has experienced self-pity, self-approval, the anguish of loss by death, the slower anguish of loss by disillusionment. These are the things which make stories. These are the things which make them whether the stories are laid in Turkestan or New Jersey. It is not lack of experience which handicaps any writer. What it is, is the purblindness which prevents his seeing, or his seeing into, the experiences he has had.

If a beginner is enough in earnest really to have studied the form he is attempting to use, he will already have put sufficient thought on some published stories to have discovered what those stories are about and how the writer has made him aware of what they are about. He will have recognized that the happenings are, individually, like beads, serving their purpose only because a cord unites them. This cord is the central and directing idea of the whole story.

A storyteller, then, is always doing two things and doing them simultaneously. He is picturing certain portions of individual lives, and at the same time he is showing some larger, some more general matter, of which those lives are the example. What the pieces of life illustrate may be a maxim or the denial of a maxim; it may be the effect of environment, race, economic placing; it may be the march of an inevitable destiny. Whatever it is, idea and incident march together. The individual figures move in the foreground of the story; accompanying them, as a man is accompanied by his shadow, appears that which they exemplify.

Which is the more important, action or idea, man or shadow, depends upon where the writer places his emphasis. In allegory, the shadow is important. In narratives of adventure, the importance of the general idea is frequently only a little greater than that of an actual shadow at midnight. It is safe to say, though, that in any story which sticks in the mind the shadow has a visible place, presentation and representation going on together.

Joseph Conrad's "The Shadow Line" is an illustration of this double progress. The young captain's obtaining of his command, his discovery of the lack of quinine, the sickness among the men, his struggle, grotesque and dreadful, against his first mate's obsession — these are happenings of absorbing interest. But at no time are readers unaware that what holds the happenings in place and gives them meaning is their effect on the captain's soul. His passage externally is from port to port. His actual passage is across that line which cuts off youth from maturity.

"Seventy Thousand Assyrians", by William Saroyan, emphasizes as definitely the dominance of idea over incident. Here the incidents themselves are related only in time. The teller chances to see one person, chances to see another, carries on certain conversations, thinks certain thoughts. What gives direction to his otherwise aimless progress is the fierce heat of a central idea. As in the allegory, the shadow is far more important than the figures casting it.

A writer finds himself possessed of an idea which worries in his brain until he arrives at appropriate actions and persons to express it; or his imagination is seized by certain people or happenings over which he mulls till their general importances grow partly clear to him. One thing or the other having happened, his story comes into being.

II

A story, then, must not only tell something; it must also be about something. In your individual story Herbert, let us say, is to be shown falling in love with Sylvia and finally winning her. Well, Herberts have fallen in love with Sylvias, have won them and lost them, since time began. Why should a reader be interested this time?

The reasons why he should be — why, decade after decade, he continues to be — have more to do with what Herbert represents, with the kind of shadow he casts, than with what he actually presents.

One of the most frequent of presentations is that of Herbert struggling against obstacles seemingly insuperable. From the time of David and Goliath, and long before, the story of the weak conquering the strong, the strong destroyed by a pebble, has been assured of readers' interest. It has been, because the reader's habit of mind in reading is identical with his habit in daily experience. If he pass a man walking along the sidewalk, one of a thousand on his way home from work, he barely sees him or sees him not at all. If he pass the same man struggling to street level from a suddenly opened crevice, clinging to a window ledge high above the street, he not only sees him, he stops to stare, cannot go on till the crisis has resolved itself — man proved stronger than obstacle, obstacle stronger than man. Those stories in which Herbert is a bank clerk and Sylvia the bank president's daughter, Herbert a divinity student and Sylvia a night club singer, draw their essential interest not from Herbert's love, which is more or less taken for granted, but from the question of whether, through the impulse of that love, he can get free of what impedes him. Can he climb out of his pit? Can he get safely down from his high ledge? What kind of hindrances he is to meet, how many, how obvious, depends upon the kind of writer you are — upon your view of life. But if your story is to hold a reader's interest, there has to be in it an implied generalization as well as a special case. The reader has to see in Herbert's success or failure an exemplification of some part of his own philosophy or to find in Herbert some vague identification with himself or his neighbor. Otherwise this strangely absorbed Herbert is merely dull to read of.

Interest produced by struggle against obstacles being set aside, the second most usual source of interest is surprise. Reduced to their essentials, the qualities of a surprise story are found, all of them, in the familiar anecdote of the Western Union messenger boy delivering his first death message. The boy — inexperienced, impressionable, afraid — lingers in front of the apartment house, pushes the bell reluctantly, hears with dread the approaching footsteps. The girl who comes to the door opens the envelope, scans the sheet, shouts up the stairs, "Ma, Uncle Henry's dead." From above comes the shouted answer, "Well, it's about time." What the anecdote does is what the surprise story has always to do, it takes a situation expected to produce one result and shows it producing another.

Thus far, analysis is easy. Unless it go farther, it is also worthless. Every year there are written probably a ton of would-be surprise stories which produce a reversal of expectation and nothing else.

Their writers have failed to take into account that, if the reversal is to accomplish its end, close on the heels of the surprise must come a recognition of the truth of what is shown. In "Rachel Mourning for Her Children", by Frances Newman, the mother of an only child sits quiet beside her son-in-law through her daughter's funeral service, bursts into unrestrained weeping only at its end. Throughout the service, she has reviewed her life — a passive child under domineering parents, a passive wife under a domineering husband, a passive widow established in the home of a domineering daughter. Never — and she is moving towards sixty — never till now has she foreseen the opportunity to select her own clothes, dispose of her own time, pour tea for her own friends from the teapot of her choice. The close of the service breaks in on her reverie; she rises and, as she does so, observes from across the aisle a widow's acquisitive eye turned full upon the grief-drenched widower.

Both reversals of expectation — her unexpected meditations, her unexpected tears — take the reader by surprise, but both, too, instantly convince him. Stories based on surprise are stories which note exceptions. Experience shows that exceptions are as true as rules. A death brings sorrow — but not always. A wedding is a scene of joy — but again not always. A mother loves her child — but sometimes too she hates it. Let it be repeated — in view of beginners' habits, it cannot be repeated too often — that surprise alone has no fictional value. The only kind capable of supporting a story is the kind which, on a second thought, ceases to be surprise at all.

Both in "Rachel Mourning for Her Children" and in Jacobs' "A Question of Habit", quoted in another chapter, surprise is bound up with situation. A story appearing in one of the later issues of *Hound and Horn* gives a useful example of surprise attached to wording only. The story records, with a luxuriance of detail, the griefs and dangers of a pioneer woman captured by Indians. The recounting of the deaths of her husband and children, of her experiences in captivity, of her escape, leaves out no particle of horror. Barely the length of a rifle shot ahead of her pursuers, she drags herself at last into the safety of a blockhouse. As she falls inside the gate, her emotions are summarized in a closing sentence. "I'm sure glad to get shut of them Indians." The understatement — the contrast between extremity of peril and inadequacy of expression — is effective only because simultaneously with the shock of it comes the reader's acknowledgment that just so she would have spoken. The rhetoric to match her torments lies in the reader's mind, not hers.

Assertion or denial of some widely accepted maxim lies at the base of many stories. A maxim is, of course, a crystallization of general belief or hope. It is based on experiences, but on selected experiences only. "Love will find out a way." "You can't keep a good man down." "Nothing venture, nothing have." — any reader can prolong the list. "Young Ames", by Walter D. Edmonds, the story of a youth who risks humiliation and loss of job for the sake of a second glimpse of his employer's niece, is founded on a whole handful of accepted proverbs. In James Stevens' "Three Lovers Who Lost", the story of the second of the three lovers reverses those same proverbs. Not only is each story acceptable to some readers, but both may easily be acceptable to the same reader, who today enjoys the exemplified rule, tomorrow the exemplified exception.

Obstacles past which the hero struggles; surprise which shows an end to action unforeseen but logical; elucidation of individual character with yet enough of the general to be in part identified with reader or reader's neighbor; fitting together of happenings to support or deny a maxim or to make clear an unsaid prophecy — any of these give a story connection and point. Some one of them you are fairly sure to discover as you turn over in mind the memorable stories you have read. When you return to your own unsatisfying one, your first necessity is to make clear to yourself what that particular story is meant to tell. Some things it will tell without co-operation on your part — something of your personal philosophy, the clarity or muddle of your thinking, the accuracy or inaccuracy of your observation. These unavoidables, however, are not your concern. What is your concern is why a piece of writing into which you have put effort is unacceptable even in the eyes of its maker. Have you a story? Or have you only a series of details, collated but not connected? If there is a story, is it ineffective because of the kind of idea which holds the incidents together? Do outworn generalizations, untrue ones, incompatible ones, lie beneath the surface of the action? What is the story *about*?

III

The question emphasized in Section II is asked of stories already formed in mind or already on paper. Earlier still, as he watches what goes on around him, two other questions tease at the brain of any would-be writer. One of these is, "What will happen?" The other is, "What would happen if — ?" According to the kind of writer you are, the first or the second fascinates you.

"What will happen?" looks, of course, to deduction from observable circumstances. "What would happen if — ?" looks to a readjustment of those circumstances through the intrusion of some deciding condition created by the writer. Frances Frost's "Piano Prelude" is a story answering the first question; Elmer Davis's "Bride of Quietness", one answering the second.

In "Piano Prelude" readers see, through the eyes of a seven-year-old child, a family of three drifting towards wretchedness and towards the child's moral ruin because of the mother's irritable and suspicious temper. The mother's outbursts, the child's answering flare-ups of bewildered anger, the timid conciliations of the father — all of these are within every reader's experience, whether at first hand or vicariously. The writer isolates happenings which concern the child, records the child's response to them; she adds no alleviations, injects no unexpected happening. Since the situation and the relations of the three members of the family are thoroughly comprehensible, what is to come — what must come —

is implicit in what is presented. The scene once set, the story moves on implacably. Not only the hours covered by it, but the years lying beyond stand out clear and unchangeable in the reader's mind.

In "Bride of Quietness" a man returns to a class reunion at the college from which he has been graduated years earlier. It is his first return. To his consternation, he discovers the magnificent boys, the potential world-changers of his undergraduate recollection, to have grown thin of hair and thick at waistline, solidified in opinions as in body. The dream-challenging girls are comfortably dowdy or stridently oversmart. So far, the second story is as much the presentation of a familiar situation as is the first. But it is not "What will happen?" which interests its writer, it is "What would happen if — ?" If, for instance, among this mob of disheartening contemporaries, there were to appear one glorious being, the class beauty, looking exactly, looking indistinguishably, except for bobbed hair and shortened skirts, as she had looked that last night in senior week — what then would happen?

Recording what will happen is a matter of observation, of analysis, of identification of writer with subject. Recording what would happen if, is the exercise of a mind awake to incongruities. One strong tie, however, unites the two kinds of stories.

Characters, conditions, and exceptions being established, a writer of either kind must stay within the limits he has set. In order to stay within them, he must do three things — keep his story to what its opening has promised; keep his people fundamentally, even if not externally, consistent; and hold his individual incidents within the bounds of that especial plausibility the story establishes. Theodore Dreiser, Ruth Suckow are writers who devote themselves with passion and with pity to stories showing what will happen. Any short story of either, followed to its end, leaves room for no conclusion but the one set down. Stella Benson, H. G. Wells, Stephen Benét, though sometimes "What will happen?" absorbs them, are still more likely to be absorbed by "What would happen if — ?"

III

TIME

"Dost thou love life? Then do not squander time, for that's the stuff life's made of."

Suggested Reading

ALBEE, GEORGE. "The Converts." *North American Review,* September, 1933

CONRAD, JOSEPH. *Youth.* Garden City, Doubleday, Doran

DE LA MARE, WALTER. "The Almond Tree." *The Riddle and Other Tales.* New York, A. A. Knopf

GEROULD, CHRISTOPHER. "The End of the Party." *Harper's Magazine,* February, 1932

HERGESHEIMER, JOSEPH. "The Dark Fleece." *Gold and Iron.* New York, A. A. Knopf

HOFFMAN, CHARLES. "It Could Happen to You." *Saturday Evening Post,* February 12, 1938

PARKER, DOROTHY. "A Telephone Call." *The Bookman,* January, 1928

ROBINSON, SELMA. "The Departure." *Harper's Magazine,* October, 1932

"SAKI" (H. H. MUNRO). "Ministers of Grace." *The Short Stories of Saki.* New York, The Viking Press

THOMAS, DOROTHY. "Three Blue Doves." *Scribner's Magazine,* October, 1929

WHARTON, EDITH. *Ethan Frome.* New York, Charles Scribner's Sons

WILKINSON, LUPTON A. "Miss Letitia's Profession." *North American Review,* June, 1934

Time

I

Sit down with a group of six people who are telling anecdotes and you will notice that at least
five out of six, and more frequently the whole
six, begin their recitals by the mention of time. "I
was going over to the store yesterday . . ." "A
funny thing happened the other night. It was just
after I'd turned out the light; it couldn't have
been more than eleven . . ." Even recapitulations of
meditations and mental conclusions are given a
time placing. "While I was getting breakfast this
morning, I was thinking . . ." "I hadn't heard from
him for a month, and I decided . . ."

Time is the inescapable factor in narrative,
whether oral or written. It is so because it is also
inescapable in life. The habit of thought bred by
living carries over to both writer and reader. If, in
life, we let go of our time leading-string even for
a moment, the result is confusion. If we let go of
it in a story, the result is confusion too, the reader's
confusion. What so overmasteringly controls ex-

istence cannot fail to control fiction; and in the writing of fiction, the treatment of time — the uses made of it for bringing out the author's intent in a story — are among the none too numerous really learnable things.

The first thing to be learned is this: Unless the writer is trying to exhibit confusion, the time of a happening in the story and the intervals between happening and happening must be kept clear in the reader's mind. Every happening has not only a time of its own but also a time relation to every other happening. What these relations are, it is essential to show.

The easiest way of showing is, of course, by mention of exact time periods.

We left the house a few minutes after noon. It was three when we got to Santa Fé; we were driving pretty fast. Nancy wanted to stay there, but we argued her out of it. We did stop, though, for coffee and sandwiches. It must have been about five when we started up the Picuris hill. That's where the trouble came. The sun was pretty nearly down. Every time we made a turn, I had to use one hand to shade my eyes, and going round those curves one-handed —

They had a fine first day of sailing weather but after that . . . a light wind directly in their eye and they hung in the wide mouth of the Bay . . . longer than Donald liked . . . They pumped an hour a day . . . In five days' time they were not a hundred and fifty miles on their way . . . One day there was hardly any wind . . . at the next dawning the northeaster was here . . . by noon that day the Mary Jane was running under reefed sails . . . At dusk he thought to heave her to . . . That night was long and cold . . . When day broke feebly, the wind had become a gale . . . The dawn was gray . . . An hour after daylight Pat took the wheel . . .

— Ben Ames Williams, "The High Heart" *

A speaker habitually locates his time with something of the exactness shown in these two paragraphs, one of them by an amateur, the other by a practiced professional hand. A beginner at writing, however, is likely to be oppressed by the frequency with which his time markers appear. "It was noon . . . ten o'clock . . . the next morning . . . a week later . . . the afternoon before" — the phrases come in such close succession that, to his own ears at least, the story is made up of identifying time statements. From some of them he tries to escape by circumlocutions but seldom successfully. On the whole, the plainest statement is usually the least conspicuous. When, in spite of plainness, mentions of time do stand out obtrusively, the difficulty

* In the *Saturday Evening Post*, December 25, 1937. Used by permission of Harold Ober, author's representative

is less often with the mentions themselves than with the planning of the story which contains them. A frequent reason for flocks of "the next minute", "the following afternoon", "when he saw her a week later — " is that the writer has not yet sufficiently labored out the arrangement of happenings in his narrative. Tags of action drift in which either are useless and so should have been left out entirely or else should have been brought into relation with events more important.

Occasionally, of course, it is the time markers themselves which are important — important for themselves, since passage of time is a crucial event in the story.

The next day she passed him in the driveway but without speaking. On Saturday he saw her with her mother, standing looking in a window on Oak Street. In the week following, he had three hungry glimpses — on Sunday on her way to church; on Monday when she came out bareheaded into the garden —

Here not the glimpses but the spacing of the glimpses are meant for the reader's remembrance. So is the spacing in Lawrence Kirk's "Study in Black and White", where the menu instead of the clock is made to give to readers their understanding of the time a change of mind requires.

Oliver at intervals glanced across the table. . . . That was his opinion while they were eating the sole meuniére. Later on, when a wing of pheasant was on his plate, he had changed his mind. . . . When the table was being cleared for dessert, he was still of the same opinion . . .

Tracing back over his own story, a writer will find "When did it happen?" a question as useful for pulling the body of the story into shape as "Why did it happen?" is useful for helping him to decide whether or not he has a story at all.

II

John L. Doughty, 322 Frein Street, was arrested at his home yesterday on a charge of embezzlement. Doughty, who has been for twenty-nine years an employe of the San Francisco branch of the Western Fidelity Company, is alleged to have admitted that, since last August, he has three times altered his books to cover peculations. Walter Harris, manager of the San Francisco branch, stated that there was no evidence of irregularity on Doughty's part earlier than August. "He was one of our most trusted employes," Harris said, "and was within two years of his pension. I cannot explain his action."

Walter Harris, manager, is fortunate. So is the reporter. Neither has to explain. The story writer must. If his story of John Doughty, embezzler, is to excite belief, it must make clear to the reader two things — first, why, after long and seemingly honest service, Doughty became an embezzler; and second, why his embezzlement began upon a certain day.

The reader, that is, needs to know what general causes, working perhaps over a period of years, undermined Doughty's integrity. He needs to know also what special cause moved Doughty on one occasion; why it was the fourth of August, not the third, not the fifth, which witnessed the final crumbling of his habit of honesty. In life, the reason for this final crumbling, the initial reasons for dishonesty at all, may remain hidden. In the story, it is the writer's obligation to bring them into view. Always, the reader of a story requires to be informed in one degree or another of the cause for a thing's happening. Always, he requires to know not only why it happened, but also why it happened at one particular instant instead of another. A cause there always is, and the difference between the working of this necessity in life and in fiction is only that in fiction both causes are brought to view.

Either general causes or special cause being insufficient, a story is sure to suffer. It is sure to suffer too if the general causes, however sufficient in themselves, are spread over what seems to the reader an impossible time period — one shorter than daily observation has taught him is needed for the alteration involved; one longer than he believes the situation or emotion presented could sustain. Whether his belief is right — if 'right' can be used in such a connection — is of no importance. A storyteller's business is so to space his happenings as to avoid the raising of doubts. "Plausibility is the morality of fiction."

There was a time in writing when instantaneous destruction of character, instantaneous upspringing of emotion, instantaneous conversions, were in fashion. There may be such a time again, but for this generation they are out of fashion. Even the quickly kindled Romeo-and-Juliet love, convincing on the stage, grows more and more difficult for the fiction writer. In any realistic story, the implication, even if not the actual presentation, of lapses of time is needed to convince a reader that an honest man has become a rogue, a rogue an honest man, and so following. "The Great Stone Face", known to every reader, makes the growth of Ernest's saintliness spread from childhood to old age. "The Dark Fleece", Hergesheimer's story of the home-coming forty-niner and his New England village, gives to the returned Jason fifteen years of absence to account for his changes in character and outlook. In

"Miss Letitia's Profession" *, the author presents his heroine with twenty-three years of odd jobs to temper the iron of her resolution, and fourteen years after that to reach a moderate fame — and, moreover, mentions each time a specific date.

Miss Letitia saw the panic of 1897 wipe the investments as blank as the paper that reposed so long in her brother's typewriter. Shuddering a little, she took in sewing. . . . Miss Letitia sewed in and sewed out. The cottage sprouted a lopsided mortgage. In 1907 Rodney's salary was raised to thirty dollars. . . . One day — it must have been about 1920 —

Time — time in plenty — is the reconciling element for almost any vital change in character or in placing. Readers' doubts on the score of possibility are destroyed by the passage of years before they are fully formed. On the other hand, brittle situations, emotions ordinarily evanescent, are instantly implausible unless they can be compressed into a limited number of days or weeks. There was once, in actuality, a grub-line rider who dropped in casually at a ranch for supper and stayed seven years. There have been, in life and in fiction, widows who, following their husbands' deaths, took for all time to crepe and silence and darkened bed-

* By Lupton A. Wilkinson. In the *North American Review*, July, 1934. Used by permission of The Editors

rooms. Such static characters now are difficult to present. Psychology, psychoanalysis, the widening spheres of interest for all humans and especially for women make them progressively more difficult. The hero of "Of No Consequence" puts a severe strain on credulity when his maker lets it be discovered that he

. . . had come to the Latin Quarter six years before, a ragged and hungry young man, his sole possessions an obsolete title and a castle crumbling in the south of France. The Quarter had been carried away by his winning manner and his amazing aptitude at defining the evils of the present monetary system. It adopted him immediately and unanimously. It fed him and lodged him, passing him on at monthly intervals. . . . Six years passed. The Quarter's original enthusiasm for its protegé had diminished . . .

Possibility has nothing to do with the case here, just as it has nothing to do with it in Ernest's coming to resemble the Stone Face or Miss Letitia's routing the burglar. It is possible that any person or any body of persons may do anything. But in a story the sole question is whether or not readers can be made to believe the thing was done. To lend credulity, however temporary, to the Quarter's supporting a stranger for six years for the reasons given is a strain on the most willing of readers.

Six days, six weeks, six months might render plausible what a six-year time interval puts quite out of court. And, in the other direction, a reader has to be far under the spell of Ring Lardner's convincing phrasing to believe that five days brings about the transformation recorded in "Now and Then." General causes require time for their working, though the time may be time mentioned only, not time actually shown in the story.

An inexperienced writer has usually less difficulty in getting his general causes safely stowed into his story than he has in doing the same with his special cause. Out of a dozen stories lacking in plausibility, three fourths are faulty through the writer's having failed to make clear why action took place on a given day rather than why it took place at all. The reason for this is, of course, that general causes are tied up with the writer's conception of his story. They stand out in his mind whenever he thinks about it. A man broken by a nagging employer, a woman rising above the aching loneliness of a Dakota ranch — these are what his story is about, these are its substance. His special cause is neglected not only because a suitable happening is hard to find, but also because he sees no necessity for finding it. To his own mind, the general cause is all-sufficient. It is worth emphasizing, therefore, that

general and special causes are separate things, are
not necessarily even of the same external pattern.
General causes may go back to the hero's infancy,
spread throughout his life, and beyond his life into
the lives of his parents and grandparents. Special
cause, the specific push into action, is one happening, placed at one definite point in time.

Everything had been as usual that morning — the
early breakfast, Frampton's sleepy departure for work,
her own mechanical gathering up of the dishes. Then,
suddenly — Ruth never knew how — she was outside
the door, she was headed towards the road, towards
freedom —

Ruth may or may not know, exactly as the writer
pleases. The reader must know. "Somehow she felt
— " "What obscure impulse moved him was never
clear — " these are phrases to be watched, signposts
of sloppy thinking. The humorous stories of Saki,
stripped as these usually are to their very skeletons,
make excellent specimens for study of both general
and special causes. In "Ministers of Grace", for example, the general causes are exhibited in the character of the Duke of Scaw, as explained in the first
paragraph of the story, and in the nagging of his
friend, as exhibited in the first two pages. The
special cause is the particular form of expression
chosen by the annoyed cabinet minister.

"No power of earth or Heaven is going to move us from our place till we choose to quit it. . . . No power of earth or — — —" *

If only the cabinet minister had not dared Heaven, he might have avoided a horrid fate. And there is something for a would-be writer to think about in the fact that, in Saki's hands, that fate did not overtake him on the first dare but on the second.

The Saki stories, though actually good guides here too, are less obvious examples of a second necessity governing the keeping of that temporary, intentionally yielded belief which a reader gives to fiction. This second necessity is that general causes and special cause, when added together, must be sufficient to account for the results they bring. They must not, when so added, be extravagantly greater than the results, they must not be extravagantly less. Here, as in every other place, the safest guide is actuality. Holding the pattern of the story up against life, can a writer justify to himself the things his characters do? Can he justify them under the conditions he has established? How would the sum of the causes he has shown act upon some person he knows? Would they make that person do what the character does? Would they make him do it

* From *The Short Stories of Saki*, H. H. Munro. Copyright 1930. Published by The Viking Press, New York

at the same point in time? Ethan Frome, heading his sled towards the Great Oak, does so for reasons no reader can deny. The general causes, spreading through his life and casting their shadows across all his future, the special cause of Mattie's nearness, her impending loss, her importunity — taken together, the sum of these things is adequate. So is it adequate with Pyecraft, bobbing about against the ceiling of his room. No reader believes, or is meant to believe in the sense in which he believes the sun will rise, that Pyecraft loses weight without losing rotundity and so unwillingly comes to emulate a balloon. But general causes and special cause fit neatly together. If there were a Pyecraft, if there were a recipe, then what the writer makes happen is exactly what would happen. Holding a story up against life means holding it all up — the character, the situation, the conditions attached to that situation.

But to fit any story, and most of all a realistic one, against life while the story is still hot in the mind is all but impossible. The fitting is a process not to be neglected, but it is one belonging strictly to revision, and one which, at any stage, taxes a writer's intellectual honesty. In daily experience, general causes are often so blurred, special cause so insignificant, that a person may say in all sincerity,

"I don't know what made me do it", "I don't know why I acted like that." There is no such comfortable retreat for the maker of an imaginary being. He has to know why his figures "acted like that", he has to make the reader share some fraction of his knowledge. Psychology — not the kind which sends white mice scampering through mazes but the kind which looks to self-and-neighbor analysis and so, at long last, to the adequate analysis in his own mind of the characters in his story — is the necessity of every writer.

It has already been said that general causes and special cause need not agree externally. None the less, a relation exists between them. Special cause must press upon the particular sore point, invoke the particular strength, which general cause has produced. Somewhere in the shipwreck scene in *Ben Hur,* Lew Wallace pauses to philosophize upon his hero's escape.

Beyond doubt every experience in life is useful to us. Where got Ben Hur the mighty muscles which saved him now? Where save in the galleys when he toiled as a slave at his oar?

Such a relation, whether for the salvation of the character or for his destruction, special cause has to bear to general ones. *Ethan Frome* is an exemplar here too. Ethan's life has been a slow starvation, an unavoidable surrender to meagerness, to querulous age and ugliness. Mattie is the antithesis of these things. Just as, in one crisis in the story, it is her expression of love for him which is the special cause, so in another it is her flushed prettiness.

But though the one cause is spiritually related to the others and is the final incitement to action, it does not therefore have to have weight in itself. Any examination of writing verifies this, and quite as much any examination of living. A neurotic, sure the world despises him, is driven to suicide by a thing so small as a child's scowling at him on the street. If the general causes for his condition have been adequately shown, then the special cause is all-sufficient, remains all-sufficient so long as it bears upon his own particular hurt.

Lack of this bearing is what usually makes impossible the lifting over into fiction of pieces of life as they stand. Except where, as in certain first-person stories, what is lifted over is the content of the writer's own mind, rearrangement, extraction of the interpretive from beneath the obvious, is always needed. A man may live next door to a caddish neighbor, hate him with a violence pushing towards murder, and yet be saved from murder by his firm's sending him to another town. That, however, is either not a story at all or is the story of something other than the hate of the two men — of some special effect of hate upon the hater, of some special emergence of his philosophy. So far as the men are concerned, the sequence of events in time — the cause and effect relation — is broken, and no story appears.

III

The place where a beginner at writing is most readily impressed with the importance of time treatment is usually in the individual passage. Usually, too, he recognizes its importance in the writing of others long before he can apply the results of the recognition to his own work. Consider the two paragraphs set below.

I had been waiting close to the telephone ever since five o'clock, expecting him to call as he had said he would. By the time the clock struck seven, I was in an agony of apprehension and impatience, my pride almost subdued to the point of calling him myself.

This is the last time I'll look at the clock. I will not look at it again. It's ten minutes past seven. He said he would telephone at five o'clock. "I'll call you at five, darling." I think that's where he said "darling." I'm almost sure he said it there. I know he called me "darling" twice, and the other time was when he said goodbye.

"Goodbye, darling." He was busy, and he can't say much at the office, but he called me "darling" twice. He couldn't have minded my calling up. I know you shouldn't keep telephoning them . . . I know they don't like that. When you do that, they know you are thinking about them and wanting them, and that makes them hate you. But I hadn't talked to him in three days . . . not in three days. And all I did was ask him how he was; it was just the way anybody might have called him up. He couldn't have minded that. He couldn't have thought I was bothering him. "No, of course not," he said. And he said he'd telephone me. He didn't have to say that. I didn't ask him to, truly I didn't. I'm sure I didn't. I don't think he'd say he'd telephone me, and then just never do it. Please don't let him do that, God. Please don't.

— Dorothy Parker, "A Telephone Call" *

So far as the information given to the reader is concerned, the first of these passages says as much as the second. It says, indeed, rather more, for it carries the situation almost to its conclusion. What it does not say, though — what it implicitly denies — is that the time period presented is of importance. In the latter passage, that importance is made obvious. By sheer bulk of words as well as by their placing and content, the reader is made to pause.

* From *Laments for the Living*, by Dorothy Parker. Copyright 1930. Published by The Viking Press Inc., New York

Recognition and emotional response follow the pause, are dependent on it.

The surest means a writer has of impressing on his readers that one passage is to be remembered, that another is no more than a bridge from one high point to the next, is his treatment of time. And time, of course, means space; in writing, it can mean nothing else. A year collapsed into a line, a minute expanded to a page — it is the minute which is memorable. What is to hold attention or to excite emotion requires to be given length, either in itself or in the passages immediately around it. What is only or chiefly for transition or for conveying of information is crowded into summary.

The wolves, first one and then another, came on stealthily towards the boy.

The stealthy, approaching shadow crept a yard nearer, then paused to lift a grey muzzle and sniff the air. The second wolf, with slobbering jaws, turned to listen. . . . A minute passed . . .

For presenting his material, a writer has two time scales, no more. He may combine them — a sentence of summary, a scrap of dialogue, another sentence of summary — but they remain but two. And whichever he uses, it is never possible for him to present either a whole happening or a whole character. The

most extensive, the most deliberate minute-to-minute presentation still is crowded with tiny elisions.
If it were not, thirty seconds would fill a book.
Where these elisions should be made, what to tell
at length, what to minimize by summary telling,
what to omit, are a writer's unending preoccupations. They are not the less his preoccupations
through coming at last to be done largely by feel
and without conscious choice.

That an important passage will usually be given
minute-to-minute treatment, that informational passages will usually be summarized — these two things
the veriest beginner already knows. But with every
careful reading of somebody else's story, as well as
with every attempt at a story of his own, the beginner discovers that these two things by no means
make up all there is to be known about the uses
of time in writing. Not what is the usual treatment
of an important passage, but how its importance may
be momentarily concealed by summary; how, by
minute-to-minute treatment, an unimportant passage may be given a factitious value or made the
screen or the announcer of one to come; to what
degree a recorded moment is affected by treatment
not of the moment itself but of those preceding or
following it — these are questions to which writers
are forever seeking new answers. If they are to

write at all, time, for them, has to be made elastic —
has to be used as whole and half and quarter notes
and rests are used by the pianist.

He broke off in his whistling. The lines under his
hand tautened suddenly, then went slack as the horses
came crowding back against the wagon. Ahead of them,
so silently that no sound of it rose above the rush of the
stream, there widened between bridge and approach a
vertical gap. Deliberately, noiselessly, the middle span of
the bridge, the empty pier beneath it, crumpled down to
meet the water. For a fraction of a second Benson
watched the gap. Then, in one complex movement, he
had flung himself from the wagon and stumbled towards
the lee side of the wreckage, the water roaring up to
meet him.

Here, it is the important moment itself which is
emphasized by detailed description. Often, though,
the important moment cannot be prolonged. The
act or speech or thought it chronicles comes and
goes between the two ticks of a clock. To drag
it out is to make it ridiculous. But to delay the
story just before it, to delay it just after, bestows
upon the moment the attention it requires and still
avoids absurdity.

"Fifteen," the elevator man announced. He clanged
the door open, clanged it shut again. She was standing

alone in the passage. Straight in front of her, a third the length of a city block away, a frosted glass door made a spot of dim yellowed light against the darkness of the walls. She could hear the elevator doors opening and shutting at higher floors, the sound softer with distance. Then the elevator was on its way down again. If it stopped at fifteen, if the man looked out and saw her standing there — Slowly, uncertainly, like a convalescent steadying herself for a first attempt at walking, she moved towards the dim light of the door.

The paragraph quoted is the opening one of the story. In it, retardation in advance of the moment serves the simplest of all its purposes. It warns the reader that something important lies beyond the closed door. It does that and it does no more. There is no characterization, no description, no disclosure of the heroine's errand. She has come up in the elevator, she dreads going farther — that is all. Behind the door may wait a usurer, an injured husband, a surgeon, an alienated child. The reader does not know. What he does know is that, by dragging out the moment before it, the writer has centered attention on the one to come.

In "The Night Hunter", by Alexander Key, the young hero of the story has slipped out, against orders, from a blockhouse besieged by Indians, to try to get meat for the hungry group inside the fort. Those within the fort hear two shots, one close upon the other.

Bush eased back upon the bar a trifle, thrust his face tight against the peephole. The moon had clouded again; the field stretching from the logs faded into an empty blackness a dozen feet away. He tried to visualize what was taking place somewhere a half mile beyond, tried to catch the first faint echo of a whistle that would tell him Ray was approaching. But he heard only the breathing of those around him and the scattered drops of rain promising a cloudburst. Thunder rolled like a regiment of drums. Lightning arched overhead, splitting the field with a white knife.*

The retardation here is set after one moment of excitement and before another — a pause not for reducing readers' suspense but for heightening it. Again, as in the earlier example, it is pause almost solely for the sake of pause. Not often, though, is retardation so closely confined to one aim. Space in a story is always precious. The paragraph used to direct attention to a given moment can also convey information, delineate character, show the birth or death of emotion, reiterate theme, enforce mood. In "Spring Thaw", Jennings, the main figure in the story, has shot a neighbor whom he had forbidden to set foot on his land.

* Used by the author's permission

The body of the shot man was pressed against the wire of the fence. The barbs sustained it for a moment, then, with a little zirr of torn clothing, it slumped down on the snow. Jennings dropped the barrel of his rifle, swung round and strode towards his cabin. He was not cold any longer. He flung his weapon up on its rack in a glow of satisfaction. O'Farrell thought he wouldn't shoot? Well, he'd shown him! He'd show any man. He guessed the place was his! Any man try to come on his place — He began moving about, putting the room to rights, replenishing the store of shavings in the woodbox. It occurred to him presently that he was thirsty, mouth dry, throat constricted. He turned towards the bench where he was accustomed to find the water-bucket and, missing it, stopped to think. Sure enough! He'd been on his way to the spring when O'Farrell — He was aware of an immense reluctance at the thought of going outside for the bucket, at the vision of himself crossing the snowy field to the spring to fill it.

Retardation, coming after the event, allows the reader an interval for the fact of the shooting to sink in. But also the paragraph gives the cause for shooting, shows the ebbing of the rage which dictated the shot, the beginnings of fear. It has a triple use, not a single one.

The value of any retardation — its worth, its rightness — can, of course, be finally judged only in connection with the situation for which it makes a pause. In "A Box of Cakes", Alesandra has asked her husband, to whom she is slavishly devoted, to bring home the cakes she has ordered for a party. They are brought not by her husband but by a messenger.

In the kitchen, Alesandra set the box of cakes on the table. She could not make up her mind whether or not to open them. She remained for a few moments trying to decide and finally set out the platters. The string was tangled, but she resolved not to cut it. Untying it without breaking the knot became for the moment the most important matter in her thoughts. She concentrated her mind entirely on the knot. It was easier not to think of anything else.

Inside, when at last the box is opened, she finds the one-line note announcing her husband's intention not to return to her. She has to find it. Any less event would make the preceding retardation ridiculous.

Observe in contrast a paragraph taken from the story of a summer visitor returning to the resort where she had once spent a vacation.

I decided to stop for a few supplies before I opened up the house. I reached the store. It was deserted. A small pile of shingles and lumber littered the dirt sidewalk. The store, in its desertion, looked smaller and dirtier than before. I walked up to the door; it was locked, and the windows were boarded up. On the door was a dirty sign, looking hastily printed, "Sea-scout Club-house moved to Jackson Wharf." Below this was still another sign, but it was the black and white perfection of a sign painter's art. "Mason and Taylor. Expert Wreckers, Reasonable Prices." Then I knew.

This time the retardation is ridiculous, for what "I" knows is only that the store is closed and its friendly and inept proprietor no longer in it. What she needs to know to justify so prolonged and de-tailed a retardation is something weighty, tragic. Lacking the justification of tragedy, the paragraph causes more expectation than it satisfies. And by the time that "I" learns, a page or two later, of the not unusual fate of her former acquaintance, whatever interest the retarding paragraph may have aroused has long been dissipated.

Thus far, the substance of the retardations quoted has concerned itself immediately with the actions or the reactions of the main figure in the narrative. The reader's eyes are turned directly on the woman who lingers beside the elevator, on the empty space into which the runner is to emerge, and so follow-ing. In "Fifty Pounds", by A. E. Coppard, the story stands still for nearly three pages while the heroine, sitting in a restaurant, listens to the talk of four clergymen at a neighboring table.

"I saw Carter yesterday," she heard one say. Lally liked listening to the conversation of strangers, and she had often wondered what clergymen talked about among themselves.

"What, Carter! Indeed! Nice fellow, Carter. How was he?"

"Carter loves preaching, you know!" cried a third.

"Oh, yes, he loves preaching!"

"Ha, ha, ha, yes."

"Ha, ha, ha, oom."

"Awf'ly good preacher, though."

"Yes, he's awf'ly good."

"And he's awf'ly good at comic songs, too."

"Yes?"

"Yes."

Three glasses of water, a crumbling of bread, a silence suggestive of prayer . . . Very delicate and dainty in handling their food they were, very delicate and dainty.*

The speakers have not been in the story before, they do not enter it again. They have nothing to do with it. The purpose they serve — their vapid talk, their impious piety — is only to underscore the heroine's mood of disgust with life.

It was fearfully hot. She knew now why the night had been so dark. The sky was no longer blue, but a dead, level white; its surface was too even to give the effect of

* Used by permission of the author, given through his representative, A. D. Peters

clouds; it was as though in the upper air the heat hung
like a pall. There was no breeze and the sea, as odour-
less as the sky, was smooth and shining like the dye in
a dyer's vat. The passengers were listless; when they
walked round the deck they panted and beads of sweat
broke out on their foreheads. They spoke in undertones.
Something uncanny and disquieting brooded over the
ship, and they could not bring themselves to laugh.

W. Somerset Maugham, "P. & O." *

Weather, temperature, scenery are agents of at-
tested usefulness for retardation. Human moods are
notably accessible to them. Landscape, in life or in
fiction, takes its color from the onlooker's feelings.
To a less degree, rain and sunshine, heat and cold
do the same. But to the amateur, such uses of externals are dangerously easy, a temptation to fine
writing, to retardation for the sake of displaying
that fine writing.

She stood motionless, looking down at the waves.
Grey, oily, beating, retreating, advancing only to be
sucked back again, futile as life itself —

He waited, staring in front of him, his mind swept
clean of thought. Years after, he could have sketched
the least detail of the scene — the avenue of pines, their
tops black against the hard blue sky, the sun in dusty

* From *The Casuarina Tree,* by W. Somerset Maugham. Copyright,
1926, by Doubleday, Doran and Company, Inc.

bars across the road between them, the dizzy round of
sparrows above the bushes, the smell of tar-weed —

Both the pathetic fallacy, in however attenuated a
form, and the "he-always-remembered" passages are
to be suspiciously regarded in the revision of any
story. Out of its context, neither of the paragraphs
above can be pronounced wrong, but both would require to be called into account while the story was
still in review. Why did she stand? Why did he?
Is the stress on either of them sufficient to meet the
emotional demand made by the writer?

Still more suspect are retardations containing ex-
traneous information. In "The Cavern", the hero
has led the girl he has seduced into the depths of a
cave and there attempted her murder. Believing he
is leaving her dead behind him, he feels his way
towards the cave's entrance.

His hand met a rough formation. "What's that? I'll
bet, by gosh, it's a stalactite. Is it growing up or down?
Let's see. No, it's a stalagmite. A stalagmite goes up . . ."

There is much more to the soliloquy, but more is
not needed to show its uselessness. Retardation is required and pressingly required, for the attempted
murder has surprised the reader almost as much as
the victim, but the content of the retardation has
to fall within the scope of the story's interest.

The example here is an extreme one, but the special shortcoming it exhibits is common enough — the thrifty attempt to make use of bits of stowed-away knowledge, bits of fine writing, quirks of observation. It should be an article of belief underscored in the creed of all beginners that anything born before, or separate from, the story to which it is attached, is doubly suspect by reason of that separate birth. Notebooks are valuable in a variety of fashions, but so far as retardations are concerned, the material committed to them is committed for burial rather than for resurrection.

It is occasionally possible for retardation before and after important action to allow the action itself to be entirely omitted.

He tiptoed across the office, opened with his own keys the door giving on the jail corridor, and let himself into the jail. The sleeping figure on the sofa did not stir as he passed. It was still lying inert and heavy breathing when he re-entered a quarter of an hour later. He crossed the room and seated himself in a neighboring armchair.

What happened in that quarter of an hour is what gives point to the entire story. Not till much later does the reader know what did happen, but he is in no danger of forgetting that some event of high importance has been prepared for.

IV

For every story, there is one decision to be made before writing begins. This is how much time, roughly speaking, the whole story is to cover — whether a day, a year, a number of years. Is the writer to follow his imaginary persons through linked series of experiences, external or mental? Or is he to concentrate on a single close-packed hour?

The decision may change as the story grows, but a decision in advance there has to be. And whatever it is, the maker of it finds one condition always with him. No matter how brief or how long the period to be presented, it is never long enough. In planning or in writing, he has to carry on simultaneously two processes. One is the freeing of his chosen time from the rest of time in which it lies embedded. The other is the reattaching to it of fragments from the past. Whether a story cover seconds or lifetimes, it has still, within a given number of words, to account for what went before its opening or to suggest what will follow its final paragraph. A naked hour, standing alone, interests nobody; its interest comes from the person experiencing it, a person who is the sum of his past. Freeing the hour from others around it means only the finding of ways to reduce the amount of information needed about that past.

The means most readily used are, of course, those borrowed straight from life. A special placing — ship, airplane, Pullman — makes superfluous some of the knowledge which a location more permanent would involve. A catastrophe does the same, since catastrophic hours are by their nature special hours.

The Reverend James Fessler awoke as if from sleep. He raised his head and strove to look about him. Instantly the unstable element on which he rested shifted its place, and he went down, gasping and struggling. He had risen and sunk again before the recollection of a boyhood spent on the Maine Coast came to his rescue. His arms drew down, fingers spread, to his sides, his head tilted, and, nose just above the surface of the water, his lightened body floated.

A main figure could not well be placed in circumstances bearing less upon his ordinary life. And yet it is that "Reverend" tying him to it which gives to the opening such interest as it has.

Dissociation is never complete. To the hour shown, threads from the past have somehow to be attached. Two stories, each dealing with an hour sharply separated from all others, may serve as examples both of the amount of detachment a special hour may have and of the ties still necessary to it.

"The Captain's Dinner", by F. H. Brennen, shows the captain of a transatlantic ship keeping his full complement of passengers in the dining hall — and thus safe from discovering that the ship is on fire — by means of a prolonged champagne dinner and a risqué floor show. The story ends with a sailor's whispered, "The fire is out, sir," in the captain's ear.

"The End of the Party", by Christopher Gerould, concerns itself with a group of four — two boys, two girls — driving towards their homes at three in the morning and at sixty-five miles an hour. The driver stoops to light a cigarette, the car swerves and strikes a man walking at the edge of the road. Its passengers, half-sobered, sick with apprehension, discover him to have been killed.

Both stories depict crucial hours. What has happened in either of them is finished, will not happen again, or at least not in the same fashion and not to the same persons. But though the hour itself is crucial, interest in it depends not on the happening but on how the happening affects the main figure — why it affects him. In "The Captain's Dinner", the required information is given by means of two of the diners, relatives of the chairman of the shipping board. From scraps of talk exchanged between them throughout the story, its readers learn that, by reputation and habit, the captain is sober, saving, austere; that these are the qualities which have won him his position and that he is jeopardizing that position now. The knowledge that he is risking his future, the wonder why he risks it, why he steps out of one set of habits into another, is what holds the reader's interest. Without a glimpse into the past, without a forecast of the captain's danger, a mere fire aboard ship and a device to prevent its discovery would hold nobody.

Along with the accident it shows, "The End of the Party" shows too that three of the four unhappy youngsters involved are of good family, well bred, not habitual roisterers. The amount of knowledge about them which is given is of the slightest, but its being given is essential. It makes the case particular, not general. Vicariously, the reader himself, his son, his daughter, has done that killing. His mind leaps forward to its wretched consequences — consequences credible because they might have come to him, pleasurable to contemplate because his experience is vicarious only.

Dissociation by means of changed location and by means of catastrophe are easy to comprehend, easy to apply, limited to special kinds of stories. More important than either is a third means, again used by the two writers just quoted. This is the placing of the main figure in a situation immediately understandable. A captain striving to protect his passengers, a speeder involved in an accident — each is a thoroughly familiar presentation. If the fire had been discovered by deck hands who, against rules and precedent, strove to cope with it themselves; if the speeders had been a terrified mother and her children, believing kidnapers to be in pursuit — in either instance, their stories must have been much more heavily loaded with explanatory matter. Of all the means of reducing the load of prior happening, the choosing of a situation comprehensible in relation to the figure involved is the most useful.

Every reader's mind — and every writer's — is full of preconceptions based on experience and on earlier reading. If a story agree with these preconceptions, it requires only the minimum of explanation. If it run counter to them, it has to justify its doing so. And the preconceptions are not necessarily static. In "To Those Who Wait", by Elick Moll, published in 1937, the opening sentence of the story, " 'I've got my job back', Jeff Miller said to himself for the hundredth time", answers most inquiries before they are asked. The main figure — an able man, a skilled worker, dazed with wonder at his escape from long unemployment — is a character calling in 1937 for no reconstruction of reader's preconceptions and therefore for no justification on the part of the writer. In 1927, justification, even paragraphs of it, would have been called for.

The beginner's fondness for striking situation leads him frequently to disregard the fact that the great bulk of experience coincides with established conceptions instead of running counter to them.

"Beastly!" murmured Lady Agatha to herself in her well-bred British voice. "Positively foul! They could well make these places higher." She removed a bit of coal dust from her cheek, regarded the handkerchief with which the removal had been accomplished, and tried again to improve her cramped position in the coal bunker. Again the unrelenting ship's beam rapped her smartly.

So far, so good. But Lady Agatha must be accounted for in that bunker, must be convincingly got into it and probably got out of it, or no story results. The greater the incongruity between person and situation, the heavier the weight of explanation; the smaller, therefore, the possibility of making the story anything other than an accounting for that opening incongruity. Manuscript after manuscript has come to grief through its writer's having mistaken a striking opening situation for a story.

But no matter how carefully a writer has chosen his opening point, no matter what the congruity between person and situation, none the less, with every story, he faces the question of how to crowd into his first paragraphs an extra ten years or so of his person's experience. Again and again in the course of revision, he finds himself with bits of information seemingly essential to his story and nowhere to dispose of them. In the passages set below are illustrated four varieties of disposal.

"This weather," thought Reggie Sheldon, pottering about in his compact hillside garden, "justifies the Los Angeles Chamber of Commerce." He raised his chunky form from the flower bed and leaned on the fence, straightening joints that no longer had the elasticity of youth. Just beyond the fence, a retaining wall kept the garden from tumbling into a dirt driveway, which disappeared around a sage-covered hill, only to reappear in the canyon below. Farther below, stretching into warm haziness, lay the disconnected mass of suburbs known as Los Angeles. Reggie knew by the mid-day calm that a cooling breeze would spring up in the afternoon. He turned, with a feeling of complacent well-being, and surveyed his handiwork. The garden was at last reaching the stage when he and Dena could enjoy it. From an ugly hillside cabin, surrounded by a wilderness of sage and sumac, they had gradually produced the pleasant cottage just visible in its setting of vines and shrubbery. They had succeeded rather well, Reggie thought, in their imitation of the little houses on the outskirts of their native city of Sydney; they should be very happy here in their life of modest retirement.

Reggie Sheldon's life had been both varied and interesting. From his earliest days, he had been a born showman. His career in Australia had begun as a professional swimmer and water polo player. Then he had managed boxers, staged a six-day bicycle race. At last he had found success as an actor. He not only gained success with the troupe, but also he met Dena, who was playing in stock. Reggie felt himself fortunate in having married not only an attractive woman, but one who stuck with him, uncomplaining, until they had amassed sufficient money for retirement. The past was now only a vague panorama in their memories, made distant by the move to America; and, having shaken off every vestige of theatrical glamor, Reggie and Dena were simple, kindly people, entertaining to each other and to their friends.

A large black sedan wormed its way up the canyon, stopping inquiringly at every intersection. Reggie leaned against the fence and followed it with his eyes . . .

On those rare occasions when Mr. Benson sat down to self-examination, there was one point on which his conscience troubled him. In most respects — as neighbor, as husband, as pattern of kindness to his four stepchildren — he could congratulate himself on a clear score, but precisely under the last item there stood recorded a secret annotation. In spite of kindness, in spite of labored efforts at affection, in his heart Benson knew he did not like the third of his wife's children.

"I can't!" Judith Worth said, sobbing. "I can't, mother! Why, he's old! Every time I see him it makes me shiver."

"It didn't make you shiver before Ted Carson came along," her mother reminded her crisply.

The two were seated on the balcony leading from their rooms, the picturesque tumult of an Italian town below them. They had been in Italy nearly three months, driven there, as Mrs. Worth now reminded herself bitterly, by the dangerous attentions of this same Ted Carson — attentions which, till his reappearance two weeks earlier, she had congratulated herself on Judith's having forgotten.

Young Druten drew a long breath. "I believe I remember it," he said. "Anyway I remember Mother bringing me here, and seeing old Fu Lin squatting below. . . . He died . . . and his body went back home in a first-class coffin.". . .

Stella Druten slipped her hand through her husband's arm . . . "It's strange, isn't it? . . . your father and Fu Lin's, then you and Fu Lin himself, and now Jimmie and little Charles . . . I wish they'd call him Fu Lin as well. That makes three generations. . . . How old were you both, honey?"

"I was six and Fu Lin was eight. . . . His father had told him to look after me. . . . He did it for the next twelve years at a stretch, right until I went to college."
— Margery Sharp, "The Second Step" *

The story from which the first excerpt is taken deals with the reappearance of a former suitor of Dena's; with his invitation to dinner, Reggie's discomfort at the dinner, and his relief at finding Dena unaffected by her one-time admirer's prosperity. This being the story, two things about its opening are evident — first, that three quarters of the explanatory material is inapposite; and second, that the remaining quarter may readily be more closely packed, made within the same space to tell much more than it now does. In contrast with the first excerpt, the second disposes of name, relationships, subject of the story, all within a dozen lines which need no explanatory accompaniment. Before the writing of his opening page, any beginner can afford to recall those time-honored requirements of the elementary composition class: time, place, person, cause made clear in the opening paragraph.

Prolonged exposition following a brief exchange of speech, as in the third excerpt, is not impossible

* In *Harper's Magazine*, June, 1934. Used by permission of The Editors

— witness "William the Conqueror" and many other stories. The escape it offers from difficulties, though, is one too dangerously easy for a beginner to take except after other openings have been attempted and found impossible. In the fourth excerpt, dialogue is used not to provide an opening for paragraphs of information but itself to include the information needed. If it cannot be used so, if solid lumps of statement must follow the exchange of a pair of speeches, then either the wrong opening point has been chosen or the story is still heavy with superfluous bits of the past.

Recognizing awkward time placings in other people's stories is rarely difficult. Finding the same awkwardnesses in your own, if once they have lodged there, is to be accomplished only by planned scrutiny. A mass of explanatory material requires to be divided into its bits, each bit tried against the whole. Is it necessary? Or is it a fragment belonging actually not to the story but to the piece of life out of which the story was pried? The Reggie excerpt — an extreme example — furnishes a field for exploration in two directions. First, which pieces can be taken away without loss? Second, what was the writer's process of thought which made those pieces seem necessary to him?

As concerns their beginnings, long-time stories meet the same difficulties as short-time ones. The first preoccupation of the writer of a story covering twenty years is exactly what it would be if his story covered a day — that of finding an opening point which presses as close as may be to the central things he wants to tell and yet leaves only a manageable bundle of earlier happenings to be disposed of. After the opening point is chosen, however, the writer of the long-time story has still to find how his particles of time can best be connected. No scene is worth minute-to-minute presentation which does not advance the main purpose of the story. And yet, in any long-time story, the gaps are as important as the presentations. The passage of months, years, in the life of a person must say something worth the saying or the narrative would not begin and end at points requiring their inclusion.

Some of the ways in which time's passage may be kept clear are discussed under Section I. But when substantial pieces of life lie between one recorded moment and the next, there is needed more than mere clarity. "Next day", once stated, may be taken for granted. "After five years", whether stated or not, must convey the sense of five years' having gone.

The simplest ways for impressing time breaks on

a reader are, naturally, the mechanical ones. As has already been noted under Section II, Hergesheimer's "The Dark Fleece" allows for fifteen years prior to the story's opening. For the months to follow, the author divides this rather long short story into twenty-two sections, each section headed by a Roman numeral. That signal of time's having passed is one no reader can miss. The amount of time eliminated, however, differs from a stretch of weeks to bare seconds. Twice, it is no more than seconds; once, the time it takes for Olive Stanes to turn, to stare, to recognize her returned and less than half-welcome lover; again, the time in which the echoes of a shouted word die on the air. The divisions, that is, do what they must always do if they are to be effective — they recognize the india-rubber quality of time and force that recognition home upon the reader.

Divisions into numbered sections, spacing, asterisks — these are markings which the stupidest reader understands. Less mechanical but almost as certain in its effect is the repeated phrase or word. Scriptural illustrations come first to mind, but illustrations are plentiful in contemporary writing as well — for example, the repeated "we pumped" in Conrad's "Youth." These devices, however, though useful for increasing the effect of a chosen time plan, are not means for the creating of that effect. Its creation is achieved only by repetition and progress of central idea from scene to scene; by enforcement, through the use of time, of the central thought, the core of meaning, of the story. Cohesion comes primarily from idea. But though it comes from idea, it may readily be destroyed by way of telling. The substance of his narrative, the thing he wants to say, may be clear in a writer's mind, and yet the parts of his story stand as separate as unwired fence posts. How to tie the parts together is the easier to see if we consider first how time ties together fragments of some individual life.

A story is to detail twenty years of a man's career — a career leading to his destruction. Through the years that you have watched some one of your neighbors pass from respectability to wastrelhood, what have been the steps of that descent? If you sum them up in "drink", "divorce", "dishonesty", or some such inclusive word, you are merely begging the question. What have you seen, or what, if the walls of his house and mind had been of glass, could you have seen, to differentiate one year from another? What would there have been to show those years either as steps or as desperate pausing places along his road?

Stories dealing with change of character or with

its marked intensification can scarcely be other than long-time stories. It is daily experience that alteration in a human being is believable only after time has tested it. Fiction, then, cannot do otherwise than support what experience has established.

V

Suggestions for improvement of beginners' work have been scattered throughout this chapter, and still other suggestions will have been drawn from study of the quoted passages and the stories listed for reading. If, however, none of these have solved your own difficulties, what should come next? If, reading your work over after it has grown cold, you find your high moments blundering past without announcement, your retardations turning to dead stops, what are you to do?

First for the high moments. The story being once completely written, read it over, making up your mind again, now that you see it all on paper before you, whether or not it has substance, whether it really is, and still is, the story you purposed to write. If it is and yet is feeble and formless in its actual writing, then one step towards possible improvement is to examine the minute-to-minute passages, questioning the content of each one. Why is this passage worth minute-to-minute presentation? Why is this one? Reduced in mind or on paper to a half-page summary, what do the three or four pages of direct treatment contribute to the whole? If they make a contribution, then is the same contribution made elsewhere, and is it worth being twice made? If it is, what variations are there in the tellings?

The high moments having been interrogated and some of them perhaps discarded or reduced to summary, the summaries themselves come into question. Reconsidered, read one after another by themselves, do the summaries actually tell all the story? Again and again in beginners' work they do. The minute-to-minute tellings are no more than addenda to them.

Walking towards the farm, he thought back over the five months he had been away, over all the hardships and disappointments of them, and how his feeling for Hilda had grown with every day. He had feared when he left that she might forget him in his absence, take up with some younger man, but now he was sure she had not, for the message which had reached him through her brother was reassuring. When finally he was inside the house and Hilda and he were alone, he was almost beside himself with joy, wanting to hold her in his arms, to kiss her, to tell her everything at once.

"Five months, Hilda! Has it seemed as long to you?" His kiss stopped her answer.

"I thought about it all the way up here. How long it had been, I mean, and how I'd missed you. There was a lot to go through, too, a lot of hardships, but being away from you was the worst. I kept wondering if you'd forget me. I thought maybe some other man —"

"I'd promised you —"

"I know you had, but when I thought about all the younger men — and then when you sent me that message by your brother —"

It is obvious that the story runs thin. It would run less thin if specific happenings, set in time, were included in the dialogue or if the dialogue itself were less one-sided; even so, minute-to-minute telling and summary parallel each other far too closely, the one scarcely more than an echo of the other.

But when high scenes and summaries have alike been examined; when, so far as you can tell, important happenings have been given emphasis, informational material stowed away, duplications sheared off, and still the story is ineffective, it is time to ask questions of the retardations. Besides retarding just before or just after an important happening, does the passage do anything else? Does it introduce information? Explain character? Glance at the story's theme? These questions being answered, there remains the all-important one. Softly read aloud in conjunction with what goes before and after, does the retarding passage fit? Is its feel right? Not too long, not too short, not ornate, not conspicuously irrelevant? The capacity to feel about his story is better for any writer than the capacity to reason, but in a beginner's revisions, reason has frequently to precede feeling and beat a path for it.

It is, of course, harder for the writer of it than for any other person to see a story's faults. You will sometimes help yourself for future stories, though not for the one in process of writing, by making a written time plan, the plan showing the moment of each action, the moments or hours elapsing between one action and the next, the reasons for the intervals. For certain kinds of stories — detective stories, stories of intricate external action — such a time scheme is an excellent thing with which to begin, and is nearly always a useful test of the first draft. For stories not of these kinds, however, it is a last resort, a counsel of desperation. The written scheme may show you what to avoid another time, but it is likely to leave you with a dead story on your hands.

IV

POINTS OF OBSERVATION

When John and Thomas, for instance, are talking together there are at least six personalities to be recognized as taking part in that dialogue . . .

Three Johns
1. The real John, known only to his Maker.
2. John's ideal John; never the real one, and often very unlike him.
3. Thomas's ideal John; never the real John, nor John's John, but often very unlike either.

Three Thomases
1. The real Thomas.
2. Thomas's ideal Thomas.
3. John's ideal Thomas.

—OLIVER WENDELL HOLMES,
The Autocrat of the Breakfast Table

Suggested Reading

ANDERSON, SHERWOOD. "I'm a Fool." *Horses and Men.* New York, The Viking Press

BENÉT, STEPHEN VINCENT. "The Professor's Punch." *Delineator*, April, 1935

BIRD, VIRGINIA. "For Nancy's Sake." *Scribner's Magazine*, February, 1937

BREYFOGLE, W. A. "The Witch Woman." *North American Review*, January, 1933

CONRAD, JOSEPH. "The Lagoon." *Tales of Unrest.* Garden City, Doubleday, Doran

DELANO, EDITH BARNARD. "Take Off Those Whiskers." *American Magazine*, January, 1938

MARCH, WILLIAM. "Nine Prisoners." *The Forum*, December, 1931

MOLL, ELICK. "To Those Who Wait." *Scribner's Magazine*, April, 1937

PERTWEE, ROLAND. "Sentimental Rubbish." *Georgian Stories.* New York, G. P. Putnam and Sons

RODGER, SARAH-ELIZABETH. "They Will Be Married in April." *McCall's Magazine*, June, 1934

SALTZMAN, ELEANOR. "First Night, Last Night." *Story*, January, 1934

SEAGER, ALLAN. "Pro Arte." *Scribner's Magazine*, February, 1937

SHEEAN, VINCENT. "Christine's Last Party." *Century*, June, 1929

UPSON, WILLIAM HAZLITT. "The Wonders of Science." *Alexander Botts, Earthworm Tractors.* New York, Farrar and Rinehart

VERNON, GRENVILLE. "Last Testament." *North American Review*, October, 1934

WOOLF, VIRGINIA. "The New Dress." *The Forum*, May, 1927

YOUNG, FRANCIS BRETT. "Cotswold Honey." *Harper's Magazine*, February, 1937

Points of Observation

I

WHEN Washington Irving presents Rip Van Winkle returning from his sleep on the mountain, he makes the presentation after this fashion:

He had now entered the skirts of the village. A troop of strange children ran at his heels, hooting after him, and pointed at his gray beard. The dogs, too, not one of which he recognized for an old acquaintance, barked at him as he passed. The very village was altered; it was larger and more populous. There were rows of houses which he had never seen before, and those which had been his familiar haunts had disappeared. Strange names were over the doors — strange faces at the windows — everything was strange. His mind now misgave him; he began to doubt whether both he and the world around him were not bewitched. Surely this was his native village, which he had left but the day before. There stood the Kaatskill Mountains — there ran the silver Hudson at a distance — there was every hill and dale precisely as it had always been — Rip was sorely perplexed — "That flagon last night," thought he, "has addled my poor head sadly."

In this passage Irving gives to the reader Rip's observations as he walks (strange names over the doors — strange faces at the windows), Rip's conscious thoughts (that flagon last night . . .), the author's summary of Rip's mood (his mind now misgave him. . . . Rip was sorely perplexed). Irving, that is, watches Rip from the outside, enters and reads his mind, offers auctorial interpretation of what is happening within him. He is in full possession of the figure he has made.

The three passages which follow chronicle the same scene but alter the point of observation.

He had now entered the skirts of the village. A troop of strange children ran at his heels, hooting after him and pointing at his gray beard. The dogs barked at him as he passed. He stared from house front to house front and up and down the length of the street. "Where am I?" he questioned at last to the nearest of the children. "There is the Hudson. There are the Kaatskills, just as I remember them, but this village is strange to me." The child did not answer, only drew farther back towards the great oak at the foot of the street.

He had now entered the skirts of the village. A child, standing at the edge of the road, saw his approach and turned to scamper up the street, frightened at his queer look. An old man of the mountain he seemed to the alarmed youngster, perhaps a troll, perhaps a crazy man escaped from some prison. Looking back at a safer distance, the child could see that the newcomer was staring about from side to side like a man wholly bewildered, while bolder children tagged at his heels, and dogs barked behind him.

He had now entered the skirts of the village. A troop of strange children ran at his heels, half delighted by his queerness, half afraid of it, themselves unaware that Rip's own unawareness of their presence held them back from tormenting him. He walked slowly, staring from side to side, bewildered, at unfamiliar housefronts. "That flagon last night," he told himself, sorely perplexed, "it has addled my poor head." The youngest of his pursuers, catching Rip's glance, began suddenly to cry, uncertain why he did so. An older brother, close on the stranger's heels, cast a "cry baby" back at the weakling, ashamed of such faint-heartedness within his own family.

In the first passage, the writer gets into nobody's mind, allows himself to tell only what could have been seen and heard by any favorably placed onlooker.

In the second, Rip is shown not from Rip's standpoint, nor yet openly from the author's, but as he appeared to one of the other persons in the story.

In the third, the writer is everywhere — outside Rip, in Rip's mind, in the minds of his followers, first collectively and then individually. He sees everything, hears everything, even recognizes emotions unrecognized by their possessors. He is omniscient.

"Rip Van Winkle" could, of course, be told not only from these but from other points of observation. The ones here given, if carried through the story, would alter it but would not metamorphose it. Told with entrance only into the mind of a neighbor favorable to Dame Van Winkle, it would become another story. Told in the first person, with Rip in the teller's role, scarcely a shred of the original would be left.

The same material, the same incidents and persons and time scheme, may make a dozen different stories according to the point of observation on which the writer decides. Points of observation, that is, are not fixed by the material. They are fixed by the individual who deals with that material. Even if the presented figure be a man alone on a rock in mid-ocean or a man inside a padded cell, he can be considered from within or from without. Neither does a writer's first consideration of his subject or first draft of his story fully decide the point from which he is to observe it. A story begun in the first person runs into obstacles and is changed to a third-person one. In third-person telling, the writer abandons one mind, chooses another, assumes omniscience, finds it clumsy, excludes it in favor of location within a single consciousness. For a beginner, the deliberate working over of a situation — the telling of it first from one, then from another point of observation — is an exercise not to be neglected. Consider the following skeleton of a story, based on a set of circumstances which nearly every one has had opportunity to watch:

X, early a widow, has taught school to support herself and her one son, Y. After Y has finished college and found a small position, X is retired on a tiny pension. Pension and salary combined keep the family solvent. A year or two later — long enough so that his mother has grown accustomed to being in command of the household — Y falls in love. X's pension is not sufficient to permit of her establishing a home alone; Y's salary will not cover the expenses of a household unless the pension ekes it out. The three people concerned, all three well-bred, well-meaning, reasonably unselfish, talk the situation over and decide on a joint establishment. It is the only decision possible if Y's marriage is not to be indefinitely postponed. The story opens after the marriage.

Here is a narrative which may end in any of several fashions, but its general course — the domestic rubs along the way, the unintended irritations, the attempts of both women to shield Y or to enlist him — these are things any writer can predicate. He can do so, not because he has seen the situation expressed in fiction but because he has watched it in life. What he cannot predicate, except as he finds the answer within himself, is from what point of observation it will be best to treat the material. Turning it over in mind, he finds it may be told in any of the following fashions:

In the first person, with one of the three figures serving as "I."

In the first person, with "I" a neighbor, a relative, an old friend.

In the first person, with "I" in any of the roles named thus far, but distant in time from the events he is relating and telling them reminiscently to illustrate some general statement.

In the third person, with access, on the writer's part, to one or two or all three of the minds concerned.

In the third person, with the writer arrogating to himself omniscience, and knowing, therefore, not only what his characters think and feel but also why they so think or feel — what forgotten childhood influences, what inherited good and ill are in control of them.

In the third person, with, again, a neighbor, relative, old friend in the teller's role.

In the third person, with the events of the story

refracted through the stream of consciousness of one of the characters.

In the third person, by means only of external evidence — such evidence as an invisible watcher, looking and listening, might collect.

All these possibilities are before a writer when he sits down to deal with the story of X and Y and Y's bride. All of them are before him when he attempts to think out his own story. In the paragraphs to follow let us analyze, and not for X and Y alone, what effect the use of one or another point of observation is likely to produce.

First for the stories told by "I": Alexander Botts, distributing Earthworm tractors over the globe and relating in reports to his firm his version of the distribution; Dr. Watson playing Boswell to a Johnson more bizarre than the real Boswell dreamed of; Marlow, looking back to the days of his first voyage — these are examples of the three "I" tellings named earlier.

A story told by the main figure in it has one outstanding advantage. It presents itself to the reader in a form to which verbal narrative has accustomed him. Like verbal narrative, it carries an extra weight of credibility. "I was there. I did it. It happened to me." It has, too, in common with all first person narratives, the advantage of a scope automatically limited. There is no question of whether or not to shift the point of observation; once taken, it is taken for the length of that particular narrative. There is also an enforced elimination of all material outside the range of the teller's attention. There is a marked reduction of time difficulties, since the story must follow the movement of one person.

Against these advantages, though, are set heavy drawbacks. The first of these is that whatever reaches the reader does so only after passage through the mind of a person himself important in the action he is recording. If the story happens to be a story of adventure, suspense is usually diminished from the beginning. "I" seeking to land an airplane, to escape from an explosion — we know that "I" did land, we know that he did escape.

A second and still heavier drawback is that, whether the record be of physical or mental struggle, "I", if he is to be taken seriously, can speak no good of himself. He cannot claim courage, high-mindedness, intelligence — any of the major virtues — unless he does so with his tongue in his cheek or under circumstances which deny the claim at the moment of its making. Alexander Botts explains in every story his own modesty, his quickness of thought, his power over people; it is possible for him to urge these excellencies on us only because what he tells is instantly refuted by the context. A figure deep in the happening of the story and yet its teller stands always to lose. Disorders of mind, flaws of temper, absurdities, delusions — for these he can be the chronicler and often is the only one who can. If readers are to feel admiration for him, he cannot be.

The greater part of the fearful night had worn away, and she who had been dead once again stirred — and now more vigorously than hitherto. . . . I had long ceased to struggle or to move, and remained sitting rigidly upon the ottoman, a helpless prey to a whirl of violent emotions . . . the corpse, I repeat, stirred —
— Edgar Allan Poe, "Ligea"

For the most wild, yet most homely narrative which I am about to pen, I neither expect nor solicit belief. Mad indeed would I be to expect it in a case where my very senses reject their own evidence. Yet — mad I am not . . .
— Edgar Allan Poe, "The Black Cat"

These two excerpts from Poe, one dealing with the supernatural, the other with the disordered mind, are too familiar to need comment. They serve only to underline the fact that depiction of madness or contests with the supernatural always permit of telling by the main character and many times demand it.

It was a hard jolt for me, one of the bitterest I ever had to face. And it all came about through my own foolishness too. Even yet sometimes when I think of it, I want to cry or swear or kick myself.

— Sherwood Anderson, "I'm a Fool" *

I was never a man who believed in a lot of sentimental rubbish, and to the best of my belief I have ordered my life accordingly. . . . I have tried to stand for my boy as an example of how a man should behave. I have always striven to show him the value of reticence, and of taking the knocks in life without raising a wail over them.

— Roland Pertwee, "Sentimental Rubbish" †

In "I'm a Fool", the "I" is disgustedly recounting the items of his own folly; in "Sentimental Rubbish", the teller's pretense of special firmness and clear-headedness in dealing with his son is denied in action as often as it is brought forward in words. With both stories, the use of "I" draws sympathy, brings the reader closer to the main figure, whether to the lad condemning the results of his own quite understandable vanity or to the father trying unsuccessfully to disguise his tenderness towards an only child.

* From *Horses and Men*, by Sherwood Anderson. Copyright 1923. Published by The Viking Press, Inc., New York
† From *Georgian Stories, 1922.* By permission of G. P. Putnam's Sons, publishers

The reminiscent story told in the first person may, of course, be told by either major or minor character. Told by a major one, the teller is, ordinarily, a character metamorphosed by time, one looking to a point so far behind him that the "I" who speaks, speaks of a being no longer himself, never to be so again, but known to him as no other can be. At first thought, this reminiscent "I" seems to have all the advantages with no outweighing drawbacks. The advantages are real — real enough to have made the form a favorite one with numbers of writers. There is, though, one accompanying requirement which usually makes this point of observation exceedingly difficult for a young writer. For the reminiscent story cannot proceed, as other stories sometimes can, merely on related action and explication of character. Looking back across life, it is essential for the looker to have learned something from time's passage. He must possess philosophy as well as recollection, and this philosophy must animate his narrative. Without it, there is no reason for his taking charge of the story.

Reminiscent telling which puts the main narrative inside a box or frame usually gives to one "I" the opening of the story, then passes it on to another.

I had known him for so long that I had all but forgotten the queer start of our friendship. I had never spoken of it — at first because I was too shy, later because I loved him, later still because it was gone from my mind. That evening, though, as we sat in our sodden bedroom, tired both of us from the long drag of the factory day — arm out, arm in, arm out again — he turned his head to look at me and, his eyes holding mine, I remembered. I could see him see me remember.

"Well, ask," he said after a little. "Ask, why don't you? I don't mind. It was like this . . ."

Thereafter the first "I" is gone, to emerge, if at all, only at the end, or for a semi-occasional sentence along the way, in order to keep the reader reminded that what he reads is being received by a listener, straight from the teller's lips.

The simplest of all the uses of the box is its use as a space saver. Time, place, immediate circumstance, relation of hearer and teller may be packed into it with an alluring economy. Children's stories provide the best examples here, especially those which run in series, the little boy returning each time to the cabin or the nursery or the library for a new recital. Aside from this obvious use, however, are other and more interesting ones which have nothing to do with space saving. Quotation sufficient to show both the content of a boxed story and the reason for the form of telling would require pages. Some examples, however — "Youth", "Heart of Darkness", "The Return", "The Almond Tree", "The Man Who Would

Be King" — are likely to be familiar to readers. Thinking back over them, most readers will pick out for themselves at least two of the many usefulnesses a box may have. These two are that it provides an incentive for telling and at the same time puts forward at its beginning the central idea which is to hold the incidents of the story together. In "Heart of Darkness", Marlow sits cross-legged on the deck of an anchored yawl, watching the placid Thames at sunset.

"And this also," said Marlow suddenly, "has been one of the dark places of the earth. . . . I was thinking of very old times, when the Romans first came here. . . . Imagine the feelings of a commander of a fine — what d'ye call 'em? — trireme in the Mediterranean, ordered suddenly to the north. . . . Imagine him here — the very end of the world, a sea the color of lead, a sky the color of smoke, a kind of ship about as rigid as a concertina, and going up this river with stores, or orders, or what you like. . . . Land in a swamp, march through the woods, and in some inland post feel the savagery, the utter savagery, had closed round him — all that mysterious life of the wilderness that stirs in the forest, in the jungles, in the hearts of wild men. There's no initiation either into such mysteries. He has to live in the midst of the incomprehensible, which is also detestable. And it has a fascination, too, that goes to work on him. The growing regrets, the longing to escape, the powerless disgust, the surrender, the hate." *

The story which follows is the story of a twentieth-century darkness; of colonizers as rapacious as were the Romans and even less permanent; of one colonizer in especial, whose surrender to the abominable is the center of the narrative. The comprehension needed for understanding his surrender, for that identification of self with the figure in a story which is a chief delight of fiction, is provided by the box. So too is the parallel between a first-century England and a twentieth-century Africa.

The box, then, underlining the special meaning of the story, has a connection with it which is spiritual, not merely the connection of like circumstance or like place. It offers also opportunity for the raising or lowering of emotion. It can soften the raw hideousness of happenings by interposing between them and the reader the veil not only of remote time, of distance, of strange surrounding, but also of a second person's interpretation. Up to a given, thought variable, point, dreadfulness on the page is a reader's pleasure. The point where pleasure ceases is where the screen made up from time and distance and unlikeness to self becomes too tenuous to hold

* From *Youth*, by Joseph Conrad. Copyright, 1903, by Doubleday, Doran and Company, Inc.

off the horror. The box is one means of keeping horror pleasurably distant. On the other hand, it is possible for it to enhance emotion by drawing a parallel between the prospective fate of the teller and that of the main figure in the story. Or it may point not in the direction of teller's fate but of reader's — "Thus will it be with all of us."

These things it is possible for a box to do. What it may not do is to provide merely a starting point for a story or a refuge for some piece of rhetoric otherwise lost to the world.

It was our first night on shipboard. Five of us, strangers that morning, old friends now, were sitting on the upper deck of the *Rantolio*. Our deck chairs were drawn close together so that we could see each other's faces through the thin, fine, silvery fog which since sunset had wrapped itself round the ship.

"You know what this fog makes me think of?" Lintauer asked when a crack in the conversation gave him room to thrust in his question. "I was on a tramp steamer in the Mediterranean once — night just like this . . ."

The chances are against Lintauer. If nothing thicker than a fog, and a recollected fog at that, ties the box to what is to follow, the writer would probably do better to come out into the open and tell his story for its own worth. Telling a story inside a box is one of the most useful of experiments, but for a beginner it is likely to be an experiment only. In the hands of an amateur, the box itself, written, polished, re-polished, loved by its writer, frequently proves more attractive than the story it encloses; frequently, too, it extends to that story only the thinnest of spiritual connection. And for lack of close spiritual connection no fine writing can make amends.

A minor figure is always an easy one to use for first-person telling. The difficulties he presents are only those connected with his plausible introduction into the scenes he is to describe and those springing from the increased chance he offers for digression. If he is more than the casual introducer who, as in Kipling's *Plain Tales,* wanders in near the beginning of a story and later is forgotten by his maker, the simplest of his uses is as the reader's representative.

"I am a little in the dark about this affair," I said. "You came to a conclusion remarkably quickly. What was it that so immediately determined the opinion of murder against suicide?"

"It was a small matter but conclusive," replied Thorn-dyke. "You noticed a small scalp wound above the left temple? It was a glancing wound, and might easily have been made by the engine. But — the wound had bled; and it had bled for an appreciable time . . ."

. . . .

Thorndyke leaned back and laughed softly.

"This is certainly an unlooked-for result," said he.

"What is?" I asked.

"Don't you see, my dear fellow? There's too much glass."

—R. Austin Freeman, "The Case of Oscar Brodski" *

The teller here receives the information that the reader needs if he is to follow the story, asks the questions the reader would ask if he were present. Sometimes, too, he enhances the reader's emotion by exhibition of his own — "I ducked down behind the bushes as the thing came past me. I could hear it whimper, and every inch of my skin was goose flesh and my heart thumped like a drum inside me" — and always he adds, as does the main figure "I", a small extra touch of authenticity. "I saw him do it. I heard it said. I was there when it happened."

Beyond these general uses, however, a minor figure, telling the story in his own person, has almost as many roles as there are stories. He may be a foil for the hero, an interpreter for him, an emphasizer of theme, a translator of special into universal. He may assert in words what the action denies or deny what the action asserts. He may, as in "The Devil and Daniel Webster", simulate on the page the

* From *The Singing Bone*, by R. Austin Freeman. By permission of Dodd, Mead and Company, publishers

homely verbal telling by which tradition passes from one generation to the next. And whenever his use is other than for the mere recording or the drawing out of information, his attitude towards events, his personality, his way of telling, color the narrative. If they do not, he is no more than waste lumber in the story.

That he will be waste lumber is, of course, one of the dangers in dealing with him. First-person telling slides so lightly from time point to time point, shakes off so many of the restrictions which pertain to "he", that a writer is tempted to use it without much thought of what the unobtrusive "I" contributes. Before a story is begun on paper, that contribution should be brought to mind, analyzed, weighed. Why should a neighbor, a son, a servant have confided to him the telling of a set of happenings not especially his? To help in answering the question, let us turn again for a paragraph to X and Y and Y's bride. If their story is to be told by a neighbor, with whom does the neighbor sympathize? How does he get his information? Will getting it involve improbabilities not involved in a more impersonal telling? What kind of individual is this neighbor? Do his prejudices, his involved emotions, his special kind of temperament give to the story some value it otherwise would not have?

These are the questions we ask for the story of X and Y and Mrs. Y. For your own story, where they are always far harder to answer, they need to be asked and reasked before writing begins. Even when the story has been born into mind as a first-person story, they still need asking. It may have been so born not because it will actually be helped by first-person telling but because of some oddity of speech of the teller's, some enticing opening scene. One way of testing the worth of first-person telling is to put yourself mentally into the position of a listener. Granted that the person, the time, and the place of telling were those shown in the story, could you, the listener, accept the teller's narrative and be convinced by it? What would you get from the teller which third-person telling would not give? Would material be open to use with third-person telling which is barred by first-person? And is that material valuable? Easy transition from scene to scene being counted out, what does "I" add? Unless it adds something more than easy transition, a beginner at fiction is likely to be safer with "he."

II

As the girls crowd in or out of the factory gate you may hear the loud hum of the novelist's art in full play. One girl is relating aloud to a friend: " 'Well,' sez 'e, 'you

come along 'o me or stop where y'are. Please yourself.'
And so she gev it 'im straight. 'It's all off,' she sez, 'an
I'm goin' straight 'ome.'" That girl, you see, keeps close
to drama. Her novel just gives you each character's most
expressive speech. Therein it resembles *The Awkward
Age* of Henry James, whom no factory girl could surpass
in the nicety of his care to tell a story the right way.

But hear how another girl treats a similar theme . . .
" 'E thinks to 'imself," says this girl, " 'we'd better know
right off,' 'e thinks, 'who's master 'ere.' An' so 'e give 'er
the office a bit stiff. 'Well,' thinks she, 'ain't I to 'ave my
bit o' pride, same as 'im?' An' so she let 'im 'ave a fair
nose-ender." This girl is a little sister of Dickens and of
Tolstoy. She "goes behind" her characters *ad lib*. She
assumes omniscience about their private thoughts.

But listen to a third girl's way of going to work on the
tale: "So don't arsk me what 'appened. I'm only sayin'
wot our 'Liza tol' me. Somethink orful, 'Liza sez it were.
'Im orf the deep end, wantin' to ply lor' and master to
the gel, 's if they was married an' all; an' 'er as bad as
'im, the cat—" In this girl the sovereign instinct of
Conrad, as a technician, is manifestly present. 'Liza is
her Marlow. Her heart tells her, as Henry James's told
him, that if she gives the story simply and wholly as it
struck 'Liza, "the terms of this person's access to it and
estimate of it contribute by some fine little law to intensification of interest."

— C. C. Montague, *A Writer's Notes on His Trade* *

* Published by Chatto and Windus, London. Excerpt used by permission of James B. Pinker and Son, author's agents

To the little sisters of Henry James, Dickens, and Conrad introduced in the quotation above, let us add one more. This is the little sister of Virginia Woolf, a sister who holds the whole story within her, sees it not as it appears to others nor yet as some one has told her about it, but only as it glimmers up from beneath the stream of her own consciousness. This fourth member having been added, we have in front of us the four ways in which stories are told. There are stories told objectively; stories where events are submerged beneath the stream of consciousness; stories where the writer sees through the eyes, or goes in and out of the conscious mind, of one or more of his characters; stories where he allows himself the freedom — and the penalties — of omniscience.

The dealer, while he thus ran on in his dry and biting voice, had stooped to take the object from its place; and, as he had done so, a shock had passed through Markheim, a start both of hand and foot, a sudden leap of many tumultuous passions to the face. It passed as swiftly as it came, and left no trace beyond a certain trembling of the hand that now received the glass.

"A glass," he said hoarsely, and then paused, and repeated it more clearly. "A glass? For Christmas? Surely not!"

"And why not?" cried the dealer. "Why not a glass?"

Markheim was looking upon him with an indefinable

expression. "You ask me why not?" he said. "Why look here — look in it — look at yourself! Do you like to see it? No! Nor I — nor any man."

The little man had jumped back when Markheim had so suddenly confronted him with the mirror; but now, perceiving there was nothing worse on hand, he chuckled. "Your future lady, sir, must be pretty hard favoured," said he.

— Robert Louis Stevenson, "Markheim"

"Markheim", as every reader knows, is a study of the working of conscience. Precisely because it is, it is interesting to observe how much of his narrative Stevenson tells by means of externals. Markheim's emotions are recorded here through the movements of his body, the changes of his face, not through entrance into his mind.

Objective treatment is, of course, hedged about by limitations — more so than any first-person telling, since "I" can always include his speculations along with what he chronicles. For many stories, for some parts of most stories, objective telling, then, is impossible. But where a story can be so told, it has the advantage of presenting information in the way that information is daily gathered — by seeing, by hearing. Even though the writer necessarily chooses what shall be seen and heard, yet the reader seems to be getting his material at first hand, seems to be left to draw his own foregone conclusions. For a beginner, attempts at objective treatment furnish valuable practice, and this whether stories result from the attempts or not.

The practice is perhaps the most valuable of all when no story is intended, when the objective account is written solely for its own sake. Observing externals, selecting the ones charged with significance, translating the results of selection into words, is the largest part of any writer's task during his early years of writing. Note in the passage following how much of character, how much of the relation between the two persons shown, is obtained by means only of external survey.

The red beard seemed to turn up at the point as the owner of it began to stride to and fro over the floor of the chamber as though he were in his admiral's cabin already. He swung round on his companion, his gray eyes very hard and bright, the burnished hair on his head thrust up like a cock's comb in his excitement.

"Hark you, Master Doughty, I can deal with the Queen's Majesty. Have no fear on that score." He walked to and fro, and Captain Doughty, a whimsical smile on his clever, handsome face, watched him.

— William McFee, "The Sun Was Over the Foreyard" *

* In the *North American Review*, May, 1933. Used by permission of The Editors

Opportunity for explication of character, for presentation of the moment's emotion by means of external description, is open to every would-be writer. The man who last week turned away from the ticket window in a rage — how did you know he was in a rage? The meek "yes" you heard some wife give back to her husband — since you could not get inside her mind, how did you discover that that "yes" meant "no"? How, still outside her mind, can you pass on your knowledge to a reader?

At the other end of the scale from the story told objectively is the stream-of-consciousness story. Here the writer enters the mind of one character and not only enters it but shuts himself within it, seeing no outside event until after it has sunk into that mind, and then seeing it not by itself but from beneath the translucent cover the mind casts over it. *Stream of consciousness* is a name well chosen, for its effect on the events of a story is singularly like the effect of a stream on things submerged in it. The pebbles in the bed of a brook show through the water, but they show with wavering outlines and colors altered. So with the happenings in a story.

She'd been a fool to go; she knew that now. It had been bad enough in the office, but it was worse when she was outside again.

All the way home, it grew worse. Eyes following her, eyes casting scorn on her. She realized how absurd her hat looked — her old winter felt hat — with the new grass in the park, new leaves on the trees. That big man over there on the park bench — he hadn't looked but he had laughed, he and the boy who sat beside him. Because he had seen her reflection in the pond, of course. That was it. Seen the hat upside down and under it her face. . . . But she could have borne all that. It was Mrs. MacFarlane she couldn't bear. Stopping her, holding out her hand, saying those things people did say — "so glad . . . such a nice day . . . never saw you looking so well" — and her own voice answering, and all the while Mrs. MacFarlane looking at the pavement, looking at the houses along the street, never, never so much as glancing at the hat, never really seeing her at all, but something in her smile, something sly, mocking, something that said, "I know about it. I know you tried for that job and couldn't get it." She freed her hand from Mrs. MacFarlane's — "so glad . . . yes — yes, of course, I'll come . . . so busy — " She was off down the street. But Mrs. MacFarlane's eyes were on her still. Smiling, smiling above those fat cheeks, they measured her — "tried for a job and couldn't get it, couldn't get it, couldn't get it." She slammed her door behind her and ran to the curtained window to look out. Mrs. MacFarlane was coming slowly down the street, stopped to speak to some one. Smiling, smiling Mrs. MacFarlane, rejoicing all the while to think that she, Amy Selfridge —

Mrs. MacFarlane, of course, does not see herself in this fashion. Probably no one else sees her so. Probably no one is spying, is mocking, is even aware of the heroine's momentary tragedy. Another mind would make of the same objects something unrecognizably different. Necessarily, then, the stream-of-consciousness story is never a story concerned with external happenings, is always one in which writer and reader alike are staring down into the stream.

Omniscience, on the other hand, allows for an observation of the mind as complete as that in the stream-of-consciousness story but allows for it from the outside. The author explores minds; he does not enclose himself within them. Exploring, however, hunting into crevices, he finds and evaluates things of which their possessors know nothing.

O'Mallen was the product of a hate. Hate had recreated and moulded him; and it had done its work well.

Up to the time the hate entered his life, he had been merely the handsomest and most turbulent member of of a turbulent and reckless family. Drinking and brawling, a month of labor with a week of tippling to follow — these were the family habits handed down from father to son. When, at the end of a breathless secret courtship, he had eloped with the only daughter of a neighbor and later been forgiven and gone to live with his wife's mother —

This is not O'Mallen as O'Mallen knows himself nor yet as his neighbors know him. It is the knowledge of a maker, looking down clear-sightedly on what has been made and naming the tool used in the making.

Mr. Buttle became as well known as any monument to the patrons. . . . He regarded pedestrians no more than we regard the red or white corpuscles in our blood streams; Mr. Buttle's business was with the carriage trade. When a car drew up to the curb, Mr. Buttle made a stately progress toward it. His was the white-gloved hand that opened its door, and later with a lordly gesture summoned its chauffeur from the parking line. . . . He it was who escorted the carriage trade through the would-be jostlers who went afoot. . . . Those people were no inconsequential atoms; they were of his own world.

Many of them indeed spoke to him by name — "Good morning, John," — though of course his name was not John. Naturally he forgave them the mistake, knowing they meant to show they were friends.

— Edith Barnard Delano, "Take Off Those Whiskers" *

Here again we have not Mr. Buttle's Mr. Buttle, who is a far more complicated and impressive person, nor yet the passerby's Mr. Buttle. What we see is the Mr. Buttle whom an omniscient eye has observed.

* Used by permission of Sanders and Conroy, author's agents.

In the opening paragraphs of a story or in explanatory summaries, omniscience is a useful tool. For the length of a whole story, it is likely to prove unwieldy. Rasselas, as readers will remember, after having had the whole world to choose from, "desired a little kingdom, in which he might administer justice in his own person, and see all the parts of government with his own eyes." A writer, having dashed about from mind to mind, from conscious to subconscious, in a few of the drafts of a story, is likely to discover that he too desires a little kingdom. The outside world with retreat into one mind has been the kingdom most writers have chosen.

With such a point of observation, the maker of the story keeps it in his own hands, observing from some invisible coign what is to be seen and heard, drawing deductions from it, moving in and out of the conscious mind of one of his persons, but letting the subconscious alone. The two examples set below are from "A Lodging for the Night", by Robert Louis Stevenson, and "First Night, Last Night" *, by Eleanor Saltzman, one a story belonging to the nineteenth century, the other to 1934.

The wind had triumphed and swept all the clouds from heaven . . . Villon cursed his fortune. Would it

* In *Story*, January, 1934. Used by permission of The Editors

were still snowing! Now, wherever he went he must weave, with his own plodding feet, the rope that bound him to the crime and would bind him to the gallows . . .

Two things preoccupied him as he went: the aspect of the gallows at Montfaucon in this bright, windy phase of the night's existence, for one; and for another, the look of the dead man with his bald head and garland of red curls. Both struck cold upon his heart, and he kept quickening his pace as if he could escape from unpleasant thoughts by mere fleetness of foot. Sometimes he looked back over his shoulder with a sudden nervous jerk; but he was the only moving thing in the white streets . . .

Lee snapped her purse shut quickly, struggling for her moment of anticipation. Ever since she was big enough to know what they were, she had looked forward to going somewhere on the pullman. Betty and Lucile and Joe Brendon had all been on a sleeper when they were still down in the grades. But she had never been outside of Indiana except twice to Chicago. And here she was now, at twenty-one, going to Des Moines on a pullman to be married . . .

She was on the last lap of her journey. At seven-thirty in the morning she would descend the car steps at Des Moines into the waiting arms of Chuck Norton. Yesterday at noon she finished her wedding dress, a new wine ensemble, just before she went back to the office for her last half-day's work. She had it with her in the overnight bag. They were to be married at noon, Chuck said . . .

She turned over on her side and pressed her face against the pillow. She ought to be tired. She and Mother hadn't gone to bed until almost one o'clock, working over her old tan suit. And Mother had tried to tell her things in her shy, inexperienced way. Lee had wanted to tell her not to mind. Girls nowadays knew more than girls of Mother's time. She'd get along all right. But she couldn't say anything past the lump of panic in her throat.

In both these excerpts, the writer is outside of his person and can record events without reference to that person's feeling — "He looked back over his shoulder with a sudden, nervous jerk." "She turned on her side and pressed her face against the pillow." — but along with this power of detached view, he has access also to thoughts and uses them as inter- preters of action, gesture, expression.

Each of the authors of the four excerpts following looks steadily into the mind of his main character. Surroundings, happenings appear as they enter these minds, but the happenings are not beneath the stream of consciousness, nor yet dragged up by omniscience from the subconscious.

. . . he suddenly asked her to marry him. For a moment or two she was silent. That didn't perturb him in the least. This serene composure in such an unusual situation was just what he might have expected from her. . . . Yet as Mr. Hopkins waited for the complaisant answer which he felt was going to give him a comfortable home, quiet company, and complete emotional security for the rest of his life, he became uneasily aware of the gathering in the dark space between them of an atmosphere . . . her voice when she spoke was not the comfortable voice whose tones he had found so soothing during the last three weeks.

— Francis Brett Young, "Cotswold Honey" *

He got up heavily from kneeling on his stiff old knees. It was bitterly cold in the little church. The dim January daylight streamed through the window, but there was no spirit in it to quicken the painted glass into life, and the altar was dull and tawdry. It might be that God and His great saints were weary of men as one wearies of watching a buffoon after a time. There was nothing but the brave flame of the candles to show that faith and hope were not wholly dead.

— W. A. Breyfogle, "The Witch Woman" †

She sat and turned the letter in her hand, dumb with despair. It was the very last letter she would ever get from him. Of that she was certain. He was gone now,

* In *Harper's Magazine*, February, 1937. Used by permission of The Editors
† In the *North American Review*, January, 1933. Used by permission of The Editors

once and for all. She had written him only once, not making an open plea but asking him to return her letters, and then there had come this tender but evasive reply, saying nothing of a possible return but desiring to keep her letters for old time's sake — the happy hours they had spent together.

The happy hours! Oh, yes, yes, yes — the happy hours!

— Theodore Dreiser, "The Second Choice" *

Later that evening Martha showed Fred the new dress she'd bought for Nancy to wear to her dancing class. She did so want Fred to feel that he shared in all she did for Nancy. But when she held up the dainty, ribboned dress, Fred (who never lifted a finger for Nancy) merely glanced at it, then complained, "But I thought Nancy asked for a blue dress. Why don't you take her shopping with you and let her choose her own clothes?"

Right then they had come very close to a break, but again Martha had been patient. "Fred, this bickering simply must stop. Don't you realize that we must work in harmony to help her develop normally? I can't understand, Fred, why you continue to balk me. Don't you care about the inevitable damage to Nancy's personality?"

— Virginia Bird, "For Nancy's Sake" †

* From *Free and Other Stories,* by Theodore Dreiser. By permission of Simon and Schuster, Inc.
† In *Scribner's Magazine,* February, 1937. Used by permission of The Editor

The ways in which the "I" in a first-person story makes himself lovable or despicable to readers have already been discussed. In third-person telling, the opportunities are even greater. Some authors — Henry James often, Conrad occasionally, Dreiser occasionally — maintain, or seem to maintain, a judicial attitude towards their creations. There stands the figure — the reader may make it what he pleases. In most instances, though, and perhaps always if readers are keen enough to draw off the cloak of seeming indifference, the maker of a figure passes on to the reader some part of his own emotion towards the being he has made. A rereading of the excerpts in this section will show how various are the paths by which he proceeds to his purpose.

Before exploring the question of which point of observation and which adaptation of that point a beginner may most hopefully try in his own story, there is one other question which should receive at least a partial answer. The question is this: A point of observation being established in the first half of a story, how readily may it be changed in the second half? What does change cost?

With certain kinds of stories, change is impossible. A first-person story can escape from its original teller only when it is told in distinct chapters. A stream-of-consciousness story may slide from one consciousness to another, but rarely can it slide out into another form of telling; it cannot because its very reason for being is that it subordinates event to mood. The same difficulty of escape from a position once chosen pertains to stories where omniscience is weighted against or for the main figure. The reader's sympathies, once placed, are rarely to be moved to a new placing. Apart, however, from these impossibilities, the wisdom or unwisdom of a change in point of observation depends entirely on its cost as contrasted with its advantages. A change uses words, always possessions to be guarded; it calls for readjustments in the reader's mind. What does it give in return?

Ordinarily, changes are made for one of three purposes — for contrast, for retardation, for the passing on to the reader of some special information. An unforgettable example of change for the sake of contrast is found in William March's "Nine Prisoners", where, by means of first-person telling, nine men, each in a separate section of the story, record their differing versions of the same hideous happening. In first-person telling, it is only by such cleavage of the story into visibly separate fragments that the point of observation can successfully be altered. In a third-person story, contrast is obtained by the writer's shifting his glance from Sylvia's mind to Herbert's. Whether the contrast is worth the shift, whether it could not be managed as well by record of externals, is a decision to be made only with the individual story in hand. In the excerpt which follows, the writer, by means of repeated changes in his point of observation, does get an effect of excited movement. He gets it, however, at the cost of jerkiness and incoherence.

"Hey!" said Golden Gate Taxies, Inc., Number 1007, as the door of his crawling taxi flew open in mid-block.

"Hey!" he called again urgently after his deserting fare, whom he saw threading his way rapidly through the opposite line of traffic. He remembered a fare he'd had Monday who acted in the same way — and him with Gladys sick at home and rent due ever since the fifteenth.

The purposeful young giant who had left him paused momentarily, turned a deeply tanned face back over his shoulder, arched a sun-bleached eyebrow, raised a commanding finger.

"Wait!" he shouted. He wasn't going to let that taxi driver hold up his search. He disappeared among the cars parked at the curb.

Number 1007 cast an appraising glance at the luggage abandoned in the back seat. He was well satisfied. It would amply recompense him for lost money and lost time. On a chance, he decided he would wait. The policeman who saw him crawl to the curb and shut off his engine remembered the regulations for taxis and moved in his direction, but changed his mind before the move was completed and became blind on the street side — temporarily blind, at least; he could change his mind again later, if necessary.

Meanwhile he of the bleached eyebrows had dashed hastily up the stairs of one of the taller buildings, his thoughts in a ferment of wonder and desire.

Office-nurse Braden, top floor of the Medico-Dental Building, was none too well pleased when a bronzed, vehement, young man burst into her little cell demanding, anxious-eyed, "Has Miss Sue Van Norden been here?"

Office-Nurse Pettit, next door, was even less gratified. She was determined to let him know that the mauve-upholstered reception room was as far into Dr. Wolfe's suite as the public was supposed to penetrate uninvited. Who did this young fellow think he was, anyway? She might have answered the question if she could have seen into his mind.

"I've got to find her", he was thinking at that moment. "I've got to! She doesn't know a soul in the city."

Miss Pettit noticed his worried look as he went out the door she had urgently requested him not to enter.

Shifts made only for retarding a passage or for introducing information into it are to be regarded doubtfully. The shift is as likely to be caused by writer's indolence as by story's necessity. In general

— though there is no "in general" applying to every writer — a beginner should try other expedients before deciding that a change from his chosen point of observation is worth more than it costs.

Practice with the various points of observation themselves, like practice with various time schemes, provides a profitable field for experiment. In the earlier years of writing, some of those experiments may well be performed on passages from the work of other people. With the excerpt from "For Nancy's Sake", for example, what two or three phrases must be removed to prevent the mother from being detestable? By the addition of what phrases could she be made pitiable instead? Would she be less detestable or more so if the story were told in the first person, the mother in the teller's role? What would happen if the father were made the teller?

Other paragraphs can be made to furnish answers for the same questions, but when a writer's own work is in question, what it usually requires first is not an examination of shifts within the story but an interrogation of the general point of observation. Some material shows at once that it can be told in one way only. But most stories, if they can be written at all, can be written with reasonable success from any of several standpoints. And yet only one of these several will bring out the full worth of the material to be used.

To gather all the important matter of a story into mind; to consider it as told in the first person, the main figure serving as "I"; as told in the third person, with entrance into the mind of the one character against whom the teller holds a grudge; as told omnisciently; as told by a teller reporting only what he sees through the wavering stream of one person's consciousness — this is a laborious process and a long one. It is, though, a process which makes the worker at home with his narrative. After the point of observation for the whole is decided beyond change, after the first draft is on paper, the time comes for considering shifts. Of each, one question should be asked in advance of any other, "Have I made this shift because nothing else will bring the effect I want, or have I made it to escape from mental effort?"

V

REPETITION

The third time's the charm.

Suggested Reading

ADAMS, SAMUEL HOPKINS. "Here Comes A Lady." *Pictorial Review*, March, 1938

CONRAD, JOSEPH. "An Outpost of Progress." *Tales of Unrest*. Garden City, Doubleday, Doran

FISHER, DOROTHY CANFIELD. "The Bradlock Chest." *The Atlantic*, February, 1935

HANLON, BROOKE. "A Man's Own." *Pictorial Review*, May, 1938

KERR, SOPHIE. "Cupboard Lover." *Saturday Evening Post*, February 12, 1938

LINEAWEAVER, JOHN. "Alan." *North American Review*, July, 1934

RINEHART, MARY ROBERTS. "The Young Visitor." *Saturday Evening Post*, July 3, 1937

THOMAS, DOROTHY. "The Home Place." *Harper's Magazine*, January, 1936

WYLIE, I. A. R. "Everything in the Window." *Harper's Magazine*, June, 1935

Repetition

"LINE upon line and precept upon precept" is a pedagogical direction applied oftenest to the teaching of morals. It is equally efficient in the study of writing, for what is to make an impression on a reader must be repeated, and re-repeated, ground into his mind by repetition. And in fiction — as also in morals — the prime difficulty is not the saying of a thing again and again, which is all too easy, but the finding of ways of saying which shall be alike in kernel and different in outer shell.

This necessity of combining difference and likeness — of saying a thing over and yet so saying it that the reader shall accept it as new — is a root difficulty of all writing. More especially it is the difficulty of the short story, where space for saying is small. Anybody can think of a basic idea for a story; the world is full of them. Or if he cannot, all he need do is to pick up a volume of familiar quotations or to unfold a daily paper. Almost anybody, having been seized by his idea, can find a beginning and an end, though not always the best ones. Where the story sags is in the middle. That sag is discoverable by every writer merely through reading over the first drafts of his own early work. Either what he is telling is reduced to anecdotal proportions, or the central pages wander off from what he has intended them to say or deaden interest by their monotony.

How much repetition a story should have, how obvious it should be, depends both on the story itself and on the audience for which it is intended. In children's stories, undisguised repetition is one of the accepted charms. Because it is, it is sometimes thought of as belonging only there. Actually, no story gets along without it. When a writer tries to express a highly complicated idea for an audience adult and sophisticated, what decreases in his story is not the number of repetitions by which he drives his idea home but only the openness with which those repetitions are allowed to force themselves on the attention.

Let us look first at the child's story.

And the Little Wee Bear said in his little wee voice, "Somebody's been sleeping in my bed!"

And the Middle-sized Bear said in his middle-sized voice, "Somebody's been sleeping in my bed too!"

And the Great Big Bear said in his great big voice, "Somebody's been sleeping in my bed! AND HERE SHE IS!"

Without a little bear and a middle-sized bear preceding the big one, making the same discovery, saying the same words, that climactic "And here she is!" would lose nine tenths of its startling effect. Its effect is startling not because it is unforeseen, but for precisely the opposite reason. It has been so long foreseen that the reader's mind has had time to move forward with the story-teller's. The discovery of Goldilocks affects him in proportion to the length and intensity of his expectation of that discovery, not in proportion to his astonishment.

And what is true of "Goldilocks" is also true elsewhere. The actually unexpected is rarely effective. A climactic event is, naturally, not itself to be repeated, but only by repetition after repetition, open or hidden, of what prepares for that event can it be given force. Mary Lamb, springing up suddenly from the placid family supper table to stab her mother, is possible in life. In fiction, she is not — not unless, tap after tap, unobtrusively, unfailingly, "There is danger, there is danger" has been hammered home into the reader's consciousness. Without that hammering home, as many a beginner's effort goes to prove, what should be horrifying is only ludicrous.

Stories devoted to the elucidation of one particular emotion or one characteristic make the easiest studies of how repetition may be used. Poe's *Tales of Horror,* ground down as these usually are to their very essentials, can scarcely be avoided as illustrations. "William Wilson", "The Pit and the Pendulum", "The Black Cat", "Premature Burial" — each one asks only that a reader shall recognize the presence and the increase of a certain kind of fear. Character is of no account in the stories. Incidents, though varied in kind and importance, yet are present only to embody the evidence on which fear is established. In "The Premature Burial", for example, after an opening devoted to consideration of those actual horrors too horrible for fictive use, the third paragraph begins,

To be buried alive is beyond question the most terrific of these extremes which has ever fallen to the lot of mere mortality. That it has frequently, very frequently, so fallen, will scarcely be denied by those who think. The boundaries which divide life from death are at best shadowy and vague. Who shall say where the one ends and the other begins?

Poe has introduced into his first page the two ideas which he means to impress on the reader's mind — the agony of being buried alive, the frequency of its happening. These two ideas having been once implanted, incident follows incident to enforce them. Pages are devoted to recording, with name and date and circumstance, examples of premature burial.

Repetition here is fully displayed; variation is not. In spite of differences in age and sex and cause of exhumation of the victims, the repeated examples have a high degree of similarity. "The Pit and the Pendulum", familiar to most readers, offers an example at once of repetition of main idea and of wide variation in the way the idea is presented. What the reader of the story is to believe in and to shudder at is the presence of prospective death by torture. The reader has no interest in the hero as a man, no acquaintance with his personality or his past. Any other hero would do as well. What is wanted is not sympathy with an individual but conviction of the reality of peril. Readers are to be convinced of that peril, to suffer vicariously from it, to be glad when it is escaped. To accomplish this end, the author must keep the peril steadily to the fore.

Keeping it to the fore by a succession of examples is not in itself difficult. A thousand bad stories have shown us that. But to keep it so without a sameness which excites first tedium, then ridicule, is less easy. To accomplish his twin ends, Poe presents first a series of dangers — an unseen pit set in the dungeon's floor; a descending blade beneath which the victim is fastened; the crawling forward of white-hot iron walls, forcing the victim towards the now visible pit. Each episode offers death, the ultimate of all terrors; each offers it in a new and hideous form. Each approaching death, too, is made to threaten not only a new kind of torment but a torment within the reach of any reader's nightmares. Each torment in turn is avoided in a different fashion — by accident, by the prisoner's own ingenuity, by the arrival of outside aid.

A reader, that is, is kept conscious of the approach to the hero of a hideous death because that approach is shown again and again. He is kept unconscious of the repetition because each time the victim is threatened in a different way and escapes by means different in kind and origin. To show a thing over and over, to make each showing different from the one following and the one preceding it — these are the two elementary requirements for all repetition. Even in a story as direct in its repetitions as is "Goldilocks", the second requirement has still to be satisfied. Chair gives way to bowl and bowl to bed before the final discovery.

But in most stories, these elementary requirements are no more than a beginning. Not only must each repetitive incident bear on the same point as its fellows and yet differ from them; each one must also fit to the scene of the story, to the temperaments, relationships, economic standing, earlier performances of the figures involved.

An example more complicated than "The Pit and the Pendulum", but again one familiar to most readers, is Susan Glaspell's "A Jury of Her Peers." Told in the third person with entrance into the mind of only one of the two women concerned, the story covers the hour in which the two wait in the house of a neighbor who has been removed to the county jail the day before on the charge of having murdered her husband. While they wait, the county attorney and the women's husbands, one of them the sheriff, search the premises for evidence which shall show a motive for the killing. Left in the kitchen while the men examine elsewhere, the women find that evidence and enter into a mute compact for its concealment.

There are three main sets of repetitions in the story: those which convince the waiting women, themselves wives, that the wife did do the killing; those which justify her in their eyes; and those which bind them together, as women, in defense of a woman. The last of the three sets is brief enough for partial quotation.

The county attorney . . . paused and looked around the kitchen.

"You're convinced there was nothing important here?" he asked the sheriff. "Nothing that would point to any motive?"

The sheriff too looked all around as if to reconvince himself.

"Nothing here but kitchen things," he said, with a little laugh for the insignificance of kitchen things.

Before the men go upstairs to the room where the killing took place, they discover that the preserved fruit in the cupboard has frozen and burst. The sheriff's wife mentions that the prisoner was worrying for fear it would.

Mrs. Peters' husband broke into a laugh. "Well, can you beat the women! Held for murder, and worrying about her preserves!". . .

"Oh, well," said Mrs. Hale's husband with good-natured superiority, "women are used to worrying over trifles."

As the three men start up the stairs, the county attorney suggests that perhaps Mrs. Hale or Mrs. Peters may come across a clue.

Mr. Hale rubbed his face in the fashion of a showman getting ready for a pleasantry.

"But would the women know a clue if they did come on it?" he asked.

Nothing is found upstairs. The searchers return to find the two women looking at the prisoner's partly finished quilt.

Just as the stair door opened, Mrs. Hale was saying,
"Do you suppose she was going to quilt it or just knot it?"

The sheriff threw up his hands.

"They wonder whether she was going to quilt it or
just knot it!"

There was a laugh for the ways of women . . .

In the meantime the women have been finding
evidence in abundance, though much of it evidence
invisible to their husbands' eyes — raggedly uneven
sewing on one block and only one of the partly
pieced quilt, a dishcloth left lying on the half-washed
table, the door of a birdcage swinging on a broken
hinge. Finally, in a box beneath the quilt squares,
they come on evidence visible to any eyes — a dead
canary, its head dangling from a wrung neck. At
sight of the dead bird, they see too the reason for
the murder, the necessity upon the wife to commit
it, her utter justification.

"We all go through the same things — it's all just a
different kind of the same thing. If it weren't — why do
you and I understand? Why do we know — what we
know this minute?"

They rip out the betraying stitches, hastily con-
ceal the dead bird in Mrs. Hale's pocket. The men
return with nothing to show for their search.

"Well, Henry," said the county attorney facetiously, "at least we found out one thing. She was not going to quilt it. She was going to — what do you call it, ladies?"

Mrs. Hale's hand was against the pocket of her coat. "We call it — knot it, Mr. Henderson." *

Of the other two sets of repetitions, those which prove the wife's guilt are of a steadily increasing weight. Their kind differs from incident to incident, their importance constantly increases. In "The Saluting Doll", by Hamlen Hunt, a story recording a Jew's recognition of the rise of anti-Jewish feeling around him, the incidents forcing home that recognition jerk up and down from trivial to large and back to trivial again with a sharpness suggestive of the movements of the doll itself, the final material witness to the truth of what the Jew, and still more his Gentile wife, had at first set down to their own anxious imaginations. But whatever the differences in weight, from the sinister reference to a brother-in-law who has 'disappeared' in Germany, to the head stenographer's casual and all unintentional "There's something about the way Jews *push* . . .", back to the screaming headline, "America Needs a Pogrom!" and on to the final menacing telephone call, no one of the happenings is apart from the story's main purpose, no two are like in form, and

* "A Jury of Her Peers", by Susan Glaspell, was first published in *Every Week*.

all of them are fitted into the framework of living of a large, affectionate, well-to-do Jewish family.

In "An Outpost of Progress", by Joseph Conrad, the wretched white in charge of the trading post hangs himself at last from the arm of the tall cross which marks his predecessor's grave. Casually, ironically, the presence of that cross, its size, its strength, its fitness as an instrument of execution, has been brought home to the reader in the earlier pages. Each time, though, it has been done in a paragraph so weighted with other importances that the mention was subsidiary and illustrative of matters which drew attention from the cross itself.

Besides the store-house and Makola's hut, there was only one large building in the cleared ground of the station. . . . There was also another dwelling-place some distance away from the buildings. In it, under a tall cross much out of the perpendicular, slept the man who had seen the beginning of all this —

Carlier went out and replanted the cross firmly. "It used to make me squint whenever I walked that way," he explained to Kayerts. . . . So I just planted it upright. And solid, I promise you. I suspended myself with both hands to the cross-piece. Not a move." *

In the first paragraph is only Conrad's habitual irony; in the second only another evidence of Car-

* From *Tales of Unrest,* by Joseph Conrad. Copyright, 1898, 1920, by Doubleday, Doran and Company, Inc.

lier's erratic puttering. Yet the two mentions have rooted the cross firmly in the reader's mind. It is there, ready to serve its sinister final purpose.

For a beginner whose stories have a habit of sagging in the middle, a first step in improvement is the analysis of some story or part of story not his own, with an eye not only to the presence of the repetitions but also to the fitting of them into the narrative. In the following paragraphs, for example, what are the points which repetition emphasizes? Are the repetitions numerous enough, varied enough, clearly directed enough? Do they avoid monotony?

The man who had not wanted to come — his name was Rinton Clarke — opened the door of his shingle cabin and looked down across the valley. It was very early but the sun was rising and through the river fog he could see the town and the grey bay beyond widening to meet the ocean in a line of tossing white. For a moment the beauty of it caught at his breath and his lungs filled in a quick gasp of pleasure. Then his face relaxed to its accustomed quiet and his shoulders again fell forward.

He left the door ajar and set about the preparation for his morning journey into the town. For four baffled years he had lived there on the hill's crest above Monterey, unoccupied, quite alone. No sunrise, no shifting of shades and colors could win him now from his habit

of resentment. As he left the house he glanced again at
the bay, grown purple in the advancing light, and
scowled his tribute to it, much as a captured Moor
might have paid tribute to the vestments of the inquisi-
tion priest. Then with his eyes upon the ground he took
the footpath down to the town.

There was only one house in the half mile between
his own and the opening of the first street. As he came
near it he checked his pace and, taking out his pocket-
knife, struck sharply two or three times on the top
strand of the barbed wire fence surrounding it. Almost at
once a girl came out upon the porch and answered the
summons by running down the path to the gate.

"You're early," she hailed him.

"I didn't think you'd be up," he acknowledged, "I
only tried it to see. I couldn't sleep any longer."

"I didn't want to lie in bed any longer either," she
amended the statement. "I'm just up, but I can't stay
in the house. Isn't it glorious?"

"It is a beautiful day," the man admitted. "I suppose
it will be like every other day, though, interminably long
and end in a grey evening."

The girl looked up at him quickly. "You are worse?"

"Not worse. It's an anniversary, that's all. I've been
here four years today — four years waste lumber." He
smiled wryly at her. "But why should one bother? Go on
in and get your breakfast. I'm going down for mine."

He nodded to her and strode on down the path. It
troubled him a little that, looking back, he saw her re-

turning slowly, droopingly, towards the house. He re-
proached himself perfunctorily.

"A part of my curse. I'd much better let her alone."
But in a moment his solicitude had veered back to self-
pity. He could have nothing that was granted to other
men, he could touch nothing —

When you turn from other people's stories to your
own, you ask yourself first, of course, what it is
in the story with which you want readers to be
impressed. There the story lies, written, before you.
What are the points — in action, in character, in
mood — on which you have meant to bear down?
Having thought what they are, you read over the
draft in front of you to make sure by re-examination
that you have hammered home what it was in your
mind to hammer. You have, let us say, a nagging
father as a main figure in the story. He is well-
to-do, liberal, devoted to his three daughters, whom,
however, he cannot even momentarily leave to their
own untroubled devices. You purpose to have his
shortcoming held up dramatically before him by
some act or overheard speech of his children, to
have him recognize it, determine on reformation,
attempt reformation, then unconsciously slip back
into his earlier habit. At the end, he is to be in the
same rut as at the beginning.

For the display of that one characteristic, can

you find ten probable incidents? Are they incidents possible to a father affectionate and well meaning? Do they fit to the economic and social standing
you have given him? Should he nag all the children
equally? Should all of them offer the same response?
And what two other pieces of knowledge concerning
the family do you have to have before any of the
questions just asked can be answered?

One writer, dealing with such a father, made
seven of his ten incidents turn upon the father's
forbidding his children to do some one thing which
all three wanted to do. He had, that is, not seven
incidents but one incident seven times shown in
only slightly different dress.

Every reader of amateur's stories has come across
examples in which the incidents used had no in-
trinsic likeness, led to no end. These are hopeless.
Where, however, as in the summary just given, there
is a coherent idea to be developed, then the working out of intervening action appropriate to that
idea is a matter chiefly of labor. This labor, this
prolonged scrutiny and testing and fitting together
of possible happenings, is exactly what the beginner oftenest refuses to do. When the excitement
of having discovered a story is past, his mind goes
no farther. To make it go farther, to center it on
the search for interpretive action is something he

feels to be beyond his powers. Often he is right. His mind, unaccustomed to discipline, cannot be commanded. But if his writing is to be other than spasmodic, his mind must sooner or later be brought under the demand of his will. One of the ways for so bringing it is to set it searching for relevant incidents. The searching is useless, however, unless each incident resulting from it is honestly examined. Because all minds, and especially those of writers, are expert at avoiding effort, some of the forms of examination likely to be useful are set below.

The whole group of repetitive incidents dealing with one idea should be read over, as a group, to determine whether they are oppressively similar in happening or wording.

Each incident should be considered separately to discover whether it fits to the external conditions — geographical, economic, social — belonging to the characters concerned.

Each should be considered in relation to the ones immediately preceding and following it. Incidents may increase steadily in importance, may shift from important to unimportant and back again. What they may not do without loss of effectiveness is to be all of approximately the same importance.

Finally, each incident in the group should be tried to discover whether it introduces discordant elements. If, out of five repetitive incidents showing the heroine losing her temper, three show her losing it because of an irritation caused by one member of her household, is that suggestion planted in the reader's brain an intentional one? Or has it slipped in only because repetitive incidents tend to become repetitions in form as well as in idea?

VI

IMPLICATION

"It wasn't so much wot 'e said as the nawsty way 'e said it."

Suggested Reading

GRANBERRY, EDWIN. "A Trip to Czardis." *The Forum*, April, 1932

HULL, HELEN. "Snow in Summer." *Story*, February, 1938

MARCH, WILLIAM. "The Last Meeting," *The Atlantic*, February, 1937

MARQUIS, DON. "Country Doctor." *American Magazine*, March, 1935

MILLER, ALICE DUER. "Plum Pudding and Mince Pie." *Woman's Home Companion*, December, 1928

RUSSELL, MARY PORTER. "Arrival." *Story*, May, 1937

STEELE, WILBUR DANIEL. "Blue Murder." *The Man Who Saw Through Heaven and Other Stories*. Harper and Brothers, 1927

THIELEN, BENEDICT. "Peacock in the Snow." *The Atlantic*, December, 1936

WIDDEMER, MARGARET. "Guidance." *Collier's*, February 10, 1934

WOLFE, THOMAS. "The Child by Tiger." *Saturday Evening Post*, September 11, 1937

Implication

IMPLICATIONS in a story are exactly what their name denotes. They are statements presented not for themselves, or at least not chiefly for themselves, but for the sake of conveying to the reader something other than the thing they say. An implication, that is, is a signpost. The post itself may or may not have value; the legend it bears must have. The post, however, may be set in any of three ways — with the legend facing the reader and thus immediately intelligible; with the blank side facing the reader, so that only after it is passed is its meaning perceived; with the legend visible, yet so worded as to be temporarily misleading. The legend can never be actually false; some suppression, some juggling with words, must always leave a way out to truth.

A set of implications meant to be immediately plain — signposts with their legends facing towards the reader — is found in "Arrival", by Mary Porter Russell.* The story, told in the third person from a child's point of observation, covers the arrival, and

* In *Story*, May, 1937. Used by permission of The Editors

perhaps an hour of time after the arrival, of a mother and child at the mountain resort where the child's father is staying.

In that hour, husband and wife meet, stroll from the stage station to the husband's cottage, go to the spring for water, stroll back towards the house. The little girl's mental picturing of her father, while she is still on the stage, has told us directly that he has been ill. In the conversation between husband and wife, we learn, also directly, that he expects his family to stay only a month, that his wife purposes to stay until all three can leave together. These things are specifically told, are part of that bundle of information and immediate action which form the outer shell of any story. Accompanying them are two sets of implications by means of which the reader learns what the real story is — things never said but abundantly made clear.

. . . father was helping them out of the car. . . . He looked terribly glad to see them, but when Joan tried to kiss him he turned his face to one side, so that she kissed only his cheek . . .

Joan wanted water, but she couldn't find a glass. "There aren't any," said father. "I had two, but I broke them." She picked up a cup then, but he called out very quickly, "Here, don't take that. Don't ever use any of the dishes with pink flowers on them."

"Why?" Joan asked him.

"Because they are *my* dishes," said father. "I've always liked dishes with pink flowers, and at home your mother wouldn't let me have any. There are just enough for me. You two will have to get along with those with gold bands."

There are more of these signposts. What they say is what no one of them puts into words — that the father is tubercular, a danger therefore to his wife, doubly a danger to a young child.

These implications concern conditions already established in the lives of the three. Beside them runs another set dealing with things to come.

"The little woman's as purty as a picture," said the driver, looking at mother. "Now I c'n see why yer wuz always hangin' around fer the mail."

Mother didn't look pleased, but father laughed. "Thank you, Jansen," he said. "Bring the bags around to the house later, will you? We're going to walk."

He took Joan's hand and mother's arm, and led them past the row of little stores, from which queer-looking people stood at the doors and stared. They wore rough old clothes, and the men needed to shave, and the women were very ugly. Father spoke to most of them and called their names.

"Jansen's a close friend of mine," he said. "Fine fellow."

.   .   .   .

Father turned in at the little house and opened the door. "Brookside Cottage welcomes you," he said.

There was a big stove inside and a lot of books and papers scattered around, and a lamp like people in the country used. It wasn't pretty at all, and back in the bedroom it was worse. There was no spread on the bed —just a red blanket on top, and it was all lumpy, as if the sheets underneath weren't smooth. Father's big, old slippers stuck out from under it.

Mother looked around and smiled. "Stand it for three months, honey?" asked father, who was watching her.

Here also the signs are turned towards the reader. He need be neither prophet nor son of prophet to let his mind run outside the boundaries of the story to the inevitable disaster which it does not tell but foretells. By means of implication, the fate of the three is carried beyond the hour to which the writer limits it. Kept within that hour imaginatively as it is chronologically, it would be too thin for any reader's interest.

"Peacock in the Snow", by Benedict Thielen,* is again a story in which the signposts bear legends immediately intelligible. The external action of the story is of the slightest. Two men, research workers at Harvard, go to call on a third, who has married

* In *The Atlantic*, December, 1936

while on leave and has returned to Cambridge with his wife.

The story opens with presentation of its most important character — winter.

Snow was deep all the way out to the house . . . the air was cold and brisk . . . we all loved the cold sharp weather . . . the dry powdery snow would be good for skiing . . . the snow and the white-painted houses looked clean and cold. . . . Everything was black and white . . . the window on which the frost crystals glittered.

The phrases quoted are, of course, not consecutive. They are interrupted by factual dialogue, by the men's arrival at the house, by description of the exotic loveliness of the Southern wife. But snow outside, drafts under doors, a reluctant furnace — throughout the story these shout aloud to any reader the thing they never say. By means of them, Henry's happiness and his wife's beauty and brilliant talent are visibly, though never verbally, doomed.

In both the stories quoted so far, the implications cannot be mistaken. They are the writer's way of telling his story. He means them to be instantly understood. Illustrations of implications intentionally misleading are found in almost any of W. W. Jacobs' humorous stories. "A Question of Habit", told by the night watchman on an anchored ship, begins with the sentence, "Wimmin aboard ship I don't 'old with" and runs through two paragraphs of critical comment on women's ways, leading to the admission, "O' course, sometimes you get a gal down the fo'c's'le pretendin' t' be a man . . ." The story being told in the first person, a reader is fairly sure to take the teller's statements as though they were the author's. When a page or two later the skipper roars at the whimpering cabin boy, "Why, you ought to be at a young ladies' school", and the boy, whimpering the more, responds, "I know I ought, sir", readers are fully prepared to accept him for the girl he is not.

It has already been said that the statement from which a reader draws a false implication must not itself be false. In "A Question of Habit", the teller never says, "Henry is a girl"; Henry himself is equally scrupulous. Having made his general comments about women, the watchman opens his illustrative story, "We 'ad a queer case once on a barque I was on", and a queer case it turns out to be. Literally taken, the assertion is accurate. So, too, when the startled skipper appeals to the cabin boy, "Don't tell me you're a girl!" the boy weepingly responds, "I won't if you don't want me to." A "yes" would throw the whole machinery of the narrative out of action. Newcomers to writing, justifying their expedients for getting a reluctant story forward, sometimes point out that, in the situation given, the person in the story would have lied. If the reader is to know the lie for a lie and know it instantly, then the person may, but if the lie is recognizable, it is, of course, no help in establishing surprise.

Several paragraphs before the end of "A Question of Habit", the hoax becomes apparent. The drawing out of the scene, seemingly to meet the needs of the skipper's slow comprehension, is really the reader's chance to relish his own almost as slow discovery. If, though, the reader chances to be a writer as well, he does not stop with relishing. He goes back over the story, observing what he may have missed at first reading. He finds that accompanying a full line of signposts which appear to read, "The cabin boy is a girl" is another line, unobtrusive but equally frequent, announcing, "He is a boy." Without this second set, the surprise at the end falls flat.

The plot of "Blue Murder", by Wilbur Daniel Steele, turns on the fact that Blue Murder, the man-killing stallion from which the story takes its title, has never been shod. That he has not is a statement saved for the last line of the story, one bringing with it a shock of surprise. And yet, along the story's course, the needed information is carefully inserted. Lost in darkness after he has crashed through his paddock fence, Blue Murder can be traced only by "the diminuendo of floundering hoofs, invisible above." The stallion gives tongue, and "to the right of it a faint shower of sparks flew like fireflies where the herded mares wheeled." Shod horses strike out sparks in their passage; unshod ones do not. The difference between the passage of the stallion and of the mares is clearly set down, but so thoroughly have misleading implications done their work that no reader is likely to observe the contrast. No reader, either, till he looks back along the course of the finished story observes the carefully placed and obscure signs pointing to the actual killer. He does observe them, though, when he looks back. He must if the surprise at the end is to be effective. An unprepared-for surprise is one of the poorest of fictional properties. By means of it, anybody can escape from any of the dilemmas of fiction, but the escape is not worth the making.

I heard his riotous retreat down the stairway. He was singing as he went and striking about with his umbrella. The crash of glass accompanied his progress and the shrieking of the other lodgers. Later we learned that he had long been confined in an asylum.

In 1872, the date of the story from which the excerpt above is taken, that unheralded "later we
learned" could evidently pass muster, could at least
get printed. It can pass muster no longer. Unless
in the story itself are the unobtrusive evidences of
madness, enough of them so that "he was mad"
is a superfluous ending, then the story is botched
work, needing redoing or abandonment.

Thus far, the implications treated have been those
important to the action of the story. They are not
always so. Frequently they pertain to character, to
economic or social placing, to the relation between
persons. Witness the opening of Alice Duer Miller's
"Plum Pudding and Mince Pie."

In a small New England village it was being said
that the four Warren boys were coming home for
Christmas. . . . That is to say, an English servant had
put two pigskin bags in a compartment on a fast train
east from Chicago. A gentleman in evening dress had
left a great public dinner after the speech of the evening,
his own, in order to catch the midnight to Boston. A
staff car had driven to the Union Station in Washington and had there deposited a colonel in the United
States Army so that he might get a train to Boston
without changing at New York. A cruiser that had seen
service in the war had come to anchor in Hampton Roads

just in time for the commanding officer to catch this same train.*

The facts are given in concise statement; it is their implication, not the facts themselves, which makes the paragraph important.

A reader's getting a bad start with a story, believing it to be about one thing and finding on the third page that his mind must be remade from the beginning, comes usually from implications introduced too late.

Rick Davis, whom Pap Johnson called, without affection, "the village brat", paused on the rocky ledge and pointed out various familiar landmarks in the valley to Rita, Pap's blue-eyed daughter. The entrance to the unheralded McCoy Caverns was at their backs, a jagged hole in the side of the rugged little mountain which formed part of Virginia's Blue Ridge.

Probably the very inaccessibility of the entrance had preserved these caves from the fate of their sisters to the north, and the much publicized Shenandoah and Luray Caverns. At any rate no one paid exorbitant prices to view the superior splendors of the McCoy; in fact, if any one was hardy enough to climb the mountain, over boulders and through brambles, just to slide down into the maw of the earth, he had certainly paid enough of a price to entitle him to look his fill. Few of the inhabitants of the little mountain community in the valley

* In the *Woman's Home Companion*, December, 1928

had ever seen the treasures of nature in those caverns. Rick was one of the few, Rita was not.

The mere thought of this day-long expedition with red-headed Rick, who had won her heart with guitar and voice, had been enough to elevate Rita to the fleece-lined heavens known only to those who truly love. And there was no doubt but that she loved this lanky, lazy mountaineer. Hadn't she thrown herself into his strong arms and wept for joy on his bony shoulder when he asked for her hand the other night? And hadn't she defended him from ridicule? Hadn't she prayed to God for his salvation? Of course she loved him.

With a negligent arm thrown across the shoulders of his bride-to-be, Rick continued to gesture across the valley with his free hand . . .

In these four opening paragraphs, the story has seemed to be that of a lovers' expedition, with suggestion of parental opposition, of possible danger from the descent into the cavern. When, a little later, the reader discovers that Rick has planned to murder his Rita inside the cave, that "little later" is quite too late. The inaccessibility of the cavern does indeed suggest danger but not that danger, any more than Rita's attitude towards Rick suggests his having already seduced her. Direct statement is, of course, impossible. The opening sentences cannot say, "Rick means to murder Rita" nor yet, "Rita is to have a child." What they can do is to establish in the reader's mind an attitude towards Rick in accord with what he intends presently to attempt instead of one which turns reader sympathy in his direction, makes him seem a victim of the father's harshness. It is to be remembered that readers begin making up their minds as soon as they begin to read. They cannot help doing so. It is when he begins to read, therefore — not on the second page, not on the third — that a reader must be guided towards the main attitudes the writer wants him to have.

Late implication, such as that in the example just given, comes from lack of practice in writing. The opening point in time having been chosen, there is so much to be said that the writer cannot pick out which are the matters finally important. Wrong implication, when it is not meant to produce a later surprise, comes usually from a writer's changing his mind as the story proceeds — comes, along with a host of other shortcomings, from the story's not having been sufficiently pondered before it was put on paper.

"Hurry up, Mary." He didn't know that this command irritated his wife a little more each time he repeated it. He didn't see her clench her teeth as she waited for the emphases to fall, each time, on exactly the right part of "hurry." Nor, if he had seen, would he have paid attention. Florence was coming in on the Panama Pacific liner today. Let's see, yes, close to three and a half hours from now she'd be in. Well, of course, it was only one hour's drive to the dock, but they wanted to be sure and be there when Florence arrived. He'd been ready for at least two hours, and why in heaven's name Mary had to gather up the laundry at a time like this was more than he could understand.

"Ma — ry, hurry up."

"Tom! Florence's boat won't be in for three hours at least. You're not helping me by hurrying me like this. These things have got to be attended to before we leave, and I can get a lot more done if you will just keep out of my way for half an hour. You haven't read the newspaper yet. It's out in the kitchen, Tom. Go on and read it."

He drew himself from the chair and, without a word, left the room. Newspaper, hell! Might glance through it, though. The front page with its three-inch bold-face headlines . . . covered with words. He read the words and they stayed words. Couldn't get beyond words. Didn't mean anything.

"Mary," he called from the kitchen, "what car are we going in?"

"The sedan, of course."

"Let's drive Florence's car. She would be sort of pleased, don't you think?"

"And Florence's bags, Tom?"

"Oh, they'd fit in the rumble seat."

No sound from the bedroom . . . maybe she was at last ready.

"Mary, you're about ready, aren't you?"

"Tom!"

. . . they left two hours later in the sedan.

There is no lack of implication here. The father's eagerness for his daughter's return, the effect of that eagerness on his wife, the grim marital discipline he endures — all these are fully developed in the opening page. Two pages later, however, the domineering mother drops from view, the father becomes the tyrant over his daughter. The story promises one thing, then presents quite another. No matter how adequately the second thing is presented, there is still a break, a need for readjustment. Poe's much quoted dictum is not always a dependable guide, but as concerns the signposts set along a story's road, it is safe to follow. Each legend must say that which will finally help out the story's purpose, its "preconceived effect." "If his very initial sentence tend not to the outbringing of this effect, then he has failed in his first step."

But while implication introduced too late springs from a writer's confusion over all that he must get told, and false implication from his having failed to think out his story, lack of implication arises usually from a mental attitude far more difficult to alter. It arises, that is, from the writer's shallow certainty that what he has said is sufficient, that from it any reader should be able to do his own inferring. Sir Walter Scott's

> I do not write for that dull elf
> Who cannot picture for himself —

is the instinctive protest of every shallow writer, who enjoys the titillation of imagining but hates the drudgery of making his imaginations clear. There is instruction to be gained by hunting out the rest of Scott's passage and discovering the minute exactness with which he proceeds to tell his readers, dull and otherwise, precisely what it is that they shall picture.

Thinness, the squeezing out from a story of all except its explicit statements, is the most difficult of all faults to remedy. Only after a considerable experience with first drafts is it possible to believe that it can be remedied, either in an individual story or in the later work of the same writer. Many times it cannot, for flat-mindedness, whether in writing or elsewhere, is a persistent characteristic. Sometimes, however, the flatness is on the page only, not actually in the mind. To try to discover which is its location, let the unsuccessful writer go over the opening pages of some story he admires, considering what is said, what is made known without saying. That done, let him subject the opening page of his own story to the same treatment. What do his words say? What information is packed into his opening paragraphs? Besides these specific phrases on which the finger can be placed, what else will the reader know when the page is ended? What are the phrases which, though they do not tell them to him, yet cause him to know these things? If phrases do not tell them, where are the omissions that do the telling?

When the beginner is very much a beginner, and sometimes even when he is not, it is useful to set down in parallel columns the information directly given and that given obliquely in the passages he is considering. It is useful also to pause after the third paragraph of a story, summarize in mind the impressions gained, and then search back for the source of each impression. Not all, nor even the greater part, of learning to write is done merely by setting words down on a page.

VII

CHARACTERIZATION

. . . and if the world had been made of machinery, he would have had the fee simple of happiness.

But to both happiness and misery there follows the inevitable second act, and beyond that, and to infinity, action and interaction, involution and evolution, forging change forever. Thus he failed to take into consideration that the lady was alive . . .

— JAMES STEPHENS, *Here Are Ladies* *

* By permission of The Macmillan Company, publishers

Suggested Reading

AIKEN, CONRAD. "Silent Snow, Secret Snow." *The Virginia Quarterly Review*, Winter, 1933

BEACHCROFT, T. O. "May Day Celebration." *The Criterion*, July, 1935

BENÉT, STEPHEN VINCENT. "The Devil and Daniel Webster." *Thirteen O'Clock*. New York, Farrar and Rinehart

BRUSH, KATHARINE. "Good Wednesday." *Harper's Magazine*, September, 1930

CATHER, WILLA. "Paul's Case." *Youth and the Bright Medusa*. New York, A. A. Knopf

CHEKHOV, ANTON. "The Darling." *The Darling and Other Stories*. New York, Macmillan

DURANTY, WALTER. "The Hit That Missed." *Collier's*, February 29, 1936

GEROULD, KATHERINE FULLERTON. "Wine of Violence." *Vain Oblations*. New York, Charles Scribner's Sons

GILKYSON, WALTER. "Debt." *Harper's Magazine*, July, 1935

HAMMETT, DASHIEL. "A Man Called Spade." *American Magazine*, July, 1932

JOHNSON, NUNNALLY. "Twenty Horses." *Saturday Evening Post*, May 17, 1930

McKENNEY, RUTH. "A Loud Sneer for Our Feathered Friends." *The New Yorker*, August 14, 1937

MAUGHAM, W. SOMERSET. "The Lion's Skin." *Cosmopolitan*, November, 1937

MAUROIS, ANDRÉ. "Kate." *Scribner's Magazine*, August, 1933

SLESINGER, TESS. "Jobs in the Sky." *Scribner's Magazine*, March, 1935. *Time: The Present*. New York, Simon and Schuster

STEELE, WILBUR DANIEL. "The Man Who Saw Through Heaven." *The Man Who Saw Through Heaven and Other Stories*. New York, Harper and Brothers

Characterization

I

THE word *character* has accumulated in English more uses than it can comfortably carry, and this whether in speech or in writing. When we say, "Bertrand has a fine character," we are likely to be referring praisefully to an actual being. When we say, "Bertrand is a fine character," the chances are that Bertrand is a figure in a story or a play. When, removing the adjective, we say, "Bertrand certainly is a character," Bertrand may be either real or imagined, but in neither case is our pronouncement flattering to him.

In a story, the so-called minor characters — or even the major ones — may actually have been given no more character than billiard balls. When one of these characterless characters is distinguished from the rest, the writer has then "characterized" his character. If he is distinguished by absurdities, he has become "a character."

Within the length of this chapter, then, where much is to be said of character, of characteristics and characterization, the word *person* is used to denote that imagined individual about whom the writer writes. *Character* is that which the writer bestows upon the person by means of the characteristics assigned to him. He makes him "certainly a character" only when he makes him a caricature.

With this preliminary establishment of terminology, we enter upon discussion of the most difficult and incommunicable of the skills involved in writing.

II

The ability to characterize is beyond doubt the most important single ability a fiction writer can possess. It is also, above all others, the one which nobody can bestow on him. A chapter dealing with characterization, if it is to avoid sham, has to begin with that regrettable admission. The utmost such a chapter can offer are the five forms of aid listed below.

It can set down warnings against those faults in characterization peculiar to amateur writing.

It can note the differences between presentation in the round, presentation in profile, and caricature —differences worth a good deal of any writer's thought.

It can point out the kind of story in which characterization is important, the kinds in which its importance is diminished or absent.

It can discuss the relation between the persons and the happenings in a story.

It can suggest devices (they are no more than that) for keeping the mind inquisitive about human attitudes and busy with finding phrases to express those attitudes.

First, then, for the warnings: Except in the rarest cases, a short-story writer should not attempt to delineate character by setting down multiplied details of personal appearance. Any writer, stopping at the nearest post-office and reading the descriptions of escaped criminals posted there, can prove this point for himself. In fiction, description is always a form of characterization; it has no other use. Either the outside look of the person is to correspond with his character and thus reveal it, or it is to differ from his character and thus produce a temporary deception. But whether for revelation or deception, no author can compel a reader to carry in mind a dozen differing details. Even when other drawbacks are disregarded, the one heavy drawback of the reader's having to alter and realter in mind his conception of the imaginary person is alone enough to discourage minute description. Still more discouraging is the waste of space, and therefore waste of reading time, involved.

Alida was fair and small and pretty, with blue eyes and yellow hair. Her skin was delicately pink and white. Her little, firm-set, red mouth, and her thin, straight nose were as small as the features of a child. Her chin was tiny too, but her eyes and forehead were as much too large for her face as her nose and mouth were small. In the plain little blue or brown or white dresses which she most affected, she looked not unlike a child. Her quick, determined walk, though, and her voice, deeper than that of most women, showed all the maturity with which twenty-four years had invested her.

The passage is not badly worded. The description does not, as amateur attempts often do, stop entirely short with outer appearance; by means of outer appearance, it does give glimpses of character. But for those glimpses, there are used a hundred and eleven words. A third of these can be deleted without loss. Two thirds can go with only slight rearrangement. In a novel, such lavish presentation is occasionally serviceable. In a short story, it is unlikely to be. The word limits which hedge about even the longest story make sure of that. Wodehouse explains of one of his persons,

She had bright bulging eyes and a lot of yellow hair, and when she spoke she showed about fifty-seven front teeth,

and so is done with her, with character in plenty set in front of the reader's eyes.

Minnie, age eleven, brown-skinned, square-templed, placid . . .

is all the personal description Minnie, age eleven, is likely to need, though in her original presentation in an amateur's story, twenty-two additional words diluted the ones here given.

In "Everything in the Window", I. A. R. Wylie presents

A heavy-built, square-headed man with glasses set sharply on a thick aggressive nose. He was somebody. Anybody could have seen that.

O. Henry's well-known hero "looked amiable and freckled" and no more, and yet no reader would be likely to complain of his being under-characterized. His predominant good temper, his simplicity, his rural upbringing are implicit in the adjectives. In actuality, freckles are by no means confined to rustics, but that fact makes them no less useful for suggesting rusticity, since the connotation of the word helps out its denotation.

For characterization, then, a particular feature, a mannerism, a line of heaped adjectives present an impression sharp and clear in the reader's mind, one that calls for no remaking. Multiplicity of details produces ordinarily only vagueness.

Unless for some special reason, a writer should not present by author's statement what is later to be proved or contradicted by his person's action.

She was witty and charming to everybody.

Her popularity sprang from her gaiety, which always made her the life of any party.

He talked, as always, brilliantly, the arrows of his wit flying sparkling about the table.

If a direct view of the person is to be given, if dialogue is to be included, the author's attributions make it only that much the harder to convince a reader who has been warned to expect much. And on the writer's side, the habit of trusting to general assertion and thus sliding away from exact presentation is one no beginner can afford to form. A figure in a story is a little like a player walking the stage. What can be told about him on the playbill is insignificant contrasted with what his own entrance, his slightest speech, can do.

This prohibition does not hold, of course, for stories told in the first person. In a first-person story, the "I" is entitled to his opinion. It does not hold, either, as concerns the recording of the effect of one character on another. "He found her witty and charming" requires no bolstering.

A writer is unwise to use the persons in his narrative, or any one of them, for ends unrelated to the story's original intent. Dorothy Canfield, in her comment on the genesis of "Flint and Fire", speaks of putting in and later taking out of her story a person introduced only to vent annoyance against a visitor who had arrived while the story was in progress. Every writer has had similar experiences. Stories in plenty and good stories too have been born out of irritation, but the irritations which occur after a story is already in progress have usually no honest place in it.

And even though a story owes its conception to irritation or to personal injury, it still requires special pondering and delay if it is not to be a waste of the writer's time. Stories by the thousand have had their inception in hurts which have disappeared by the time the third page is written. Even if the hurt continues unabated, it is still likely to pull the narrative out of its course, bend it towards the justifying of its injured creator. The author who caused his jilted heroine to thrust into her fiction a foiled and publicly disgraced adventuress "so like her rival that, at the last moment, she was terrified and added a few disfiguring moles" was exploiting an all but universal tendency. Personal annoyances, personal grievances need to be revalued in terms other than the personal before they are ready for use. Impersonal emotional disturbances — generous indignations, pities, admirations — are the very yeast of fiction, but even with these, deliberation has its advantages. If, its first draft being completed, every story born of a sudden intense emotion were laid away for cooling, some few admirable things might be lost, but the saving of time now squandered on the working and reworking of the impossible would be enormous. Wordsworth's "emotion recollected in tranquility" has its applications outside the verse. Especially it has its application to the presentation of character, the most emotion-stirring part of any writer's work.

The prohibitions just set down are, naturally, not absolute. There are occasional exceptions to every one, just as there are exceptions to any statement, positive or negative, which can be made about writing. But the lapses here pointed out are those to which beginners are prone. Added together, the negatives come at last to an affirmative: The writer shall deal honestly with his human material. He deals with it in what terms he pleases — in terms of fantasy, idealization, mockery, exact representation — but each of his persons requires to be made of one piece, and this means that each must have become of a piece in his own mind before writing is attempted. Time for scrutiny, for re-evaluation, for winding the mind about its subject, is needed at every stage in fiction writing, but most of all is it needed in the consideration of character. Of all the "Thou shalt not's", the inclusive one is "Thou shalt not begin without long prior meditation."

III

The suggestions given in the preceding section can be tested against the background of almost any story the writer happens to have read. Before their efficacy in regard to his own stories can be decided, two other decisions must be reached, one of which is whether the persons he is about to present, if they are to be characterized at all, are to be presented in the round, in profile, or by caricature. In terms borrowed from another art, is the writer attempting a statue, a bas-relief, a cartoon?

Nobody supposes a bas-relief to be the whole man, but it may suggest the man, emphasize his salient point, as effectively as does a fuller representation. It is sometimes even more effective, since it is necessarily greatly simplified. In the same fashion, presentation of a person through some one trait is often effective by reason of its single-minded directness of aim. Presentation of a trait, however, and the presentation which attempts the encompassing in words of a whole person are different acts — acts different in kind, not only in degree. They presuppose different approaches on the writer's part to his story, a different attitude towards the person he is presenting, a different purpose as regards his readers. If a beginner has not already thought out these differences, he would do well to pause a long time over each of the phrases just used.

For the differences involved are far more than merely those which concern amount of selection. Selection goes on, and goes on unceasingly, in both processes, though it is necessarily a narrower one when only a trait is to be shown. The gulf between the two presentations, however, is not that the writer takes this and rejects that in the one instance or in the other. The important difference lies in what he does, or purposes to do, with the material remaining in his hands after selection.

When his attempt is to encompass a person, his attention is centered on making his readers acquainted with that person. When he is presenting a single trait dressed out in human form, his attention is on making his readers, all his readers, feel for that personified trait one particular and limited emotion. For illustration of this difference, let us look at two stories, "Paul's Case", by Willa Cather, and "Good Wednesday", by Katharine Brush.

Paul, a lad of high-school age, is, objectively viewed, a thoroughly bad lot. He is a torment at school, an anxiety at home, a persistent liar, a worshiper of false values, finally a thief and a suicide. His teachers unanimously dislike him, their dislike built up on the boy's glitteringly defiant manner, on the unconcealed contempt with which he meets them. Readers, however, even from the opening of the story, are less unanimous than are the teachers. Paul is disagreeable always, is repulsive always. But among ten individuals following his story, there may readily be ten different shades of feeling towards him. Pity may predominate, or sympathy, or sheer distaste. The weight of his shortcomings may rest, in the reader's mind, on Paul himself, on his neighborhood, on society at large, even on Destiny. The same unhappy lad, the same appearance, actions, gestures, speeches are placed before all; the reactions are widely different.

Willa Cather, that is, is engaged in presenting a human being. Paul is shown in the round. So is Ethan in "Ethan Frome." So — and with an amazing economy — are Major and Mrs. Monarch in Henry James' "The Real Thing."

This is not to say that, with any one of these stories, there does not exist a common denominator in the feelings of readers towards the persons characterized. Such a common denominator is always present. But it is that and no more. Enough is shown to enable a reader to make his individual evaluation — one made in the terms of his own experiences and what his temperament has made of those experiences. Within the boundaries of one family, the father may carry Mulvaney warm in his heart, the mother relegate "Soldiers Three" to a high shelf to prevent the children from meeting him, and the young son, having found him there, push the book back into place, voting Mulvaney a bore.

When what is presented is not a character but an embodied trait, these differences of feeling do not exist. The writer has decided in advance how all readers shall feel; he presents only what must make them feel so. In "Good Wednesday", a middle-aged hairdresser is depicted as she appears from the time she gets up in the morning till she starts for prayer meeting at night. Throughout the day, she goes from client to client in the small town where she practices. With each client, she leaves some morsel of malicious gossip, some virulently harmful deduction or invention. From each, she takes away a bit to be enlarged and embroidered for later use. Liking for her on any reader's part is out of the question. So is pity. So is the shifting from her of responsibility for her acts — a shifting unconsciously performed by many readers of "Paul's case." Presumably, with the hairdresser quite as much as with Paul, there are reasons why she is as she is; presumably there may be moments when she is otherwise. But no hint of such moments or such causes enters the story. It is not a person, it is a trait, and that of petty malignity, which moves convincingly through the pages.

A second difference between presentation of character and that of trait is that presentation of character involves usually no moral judgment on the part of either writer or reader. Witness Mulvaney in "The Courting of Dinah Shadd." Witness Rip Van Winkle. Even the horrid beings who inhabit

Katherine Fullerton Gerould's "Wine of Violence" are not beings open to inevitable condemnation. The reader shudders at them, but the causes for their actions, the impulsions which left them helpless in the hold of hates stronger than they, speak up in their behalf, even against a performance which itself is outside the range of human sympathy.

Successful presentation of a trait, on the other hand, involves on the author's part not only determination of exactly how readers shall feel but also determination to make that feeling righteous as well as unanimous. The author's selection from his person's actions has therefore to be limited even more strictly than the trait itself demands. Consistency is his first requirement. Everything — act, speech, gesture, thoughts — must enforce not only the trait to be shown but also the reader's detestation or admiration of that trait. For presentation of character, on the other hand, selection, though it has always to be made, yet has a wide range. No story can compass a man. But the base on which the writer builds is narrow in the one instance, broad in the other.

For caricature, the base is much the same as for presentation of a trait. Selection is equally narrow, but the trait presented is so enhanced as to be implausible except within the special atmosphere provided by the story. Miss Baxter, in "Good Wednesday", can be transferred out of her story. "So-and-so is like that", is one of the most usual of readers' reactions. There is more difficulty in transferring Gash Tuttle, hero of Irvin Cobb's "Smart Aleck", from page to life. There is still more difficulty in transferring the hero of Nunnally Johnson's "Twenty Horses." Inside the story he can produce the momentary credulity needed for enjoyment, but no admirer places him in an actual scene, compares him with a living being. A caricature demands not only selection as rigid as that required for a personified trait, but also a surrounding and magnifying atmosphere outside of which the figure cannot live.

Which, then, have you meant to present in your story? Which have you presented?

As between caricature on the one hand and either character or personified trait on the other, distinction is not difficult. Unless he be extremely inexpert, the writer who is drawing a caricature knows he is doing so. He knows his figure will have reality to the reader only inside the setting, the thickened or rarefied air, he has intentionally created for him. If, in your own instance, however, you have doubts —if, that is, you think yourself to have drawn a character but, at uneasy later reading, suspect an unintended caricature — the first and easiest of tests is the transference just suggested. In your own mind, can the imaginary figure be set down in everyday surroundings? Can he walk up your front steps, carry on his recorded conversation in your living room, and not be adjudged insane by any listener? To such readers as have met him, Mr. Quilp is probably as fully alive as Becky Sharp, but, unlike Becky, he cannot be made to travel. His uncanny river-edge residence, his saucepan of boiling gin, the dog in the lane which "lives on the left side but usually lurks on the right", are essential to his existence. He is a special figure, made for special purpose, allegorical as all caricatures are allegorical, and not at any moment to be taken for actual.

If, then, there is a possibility that the figure you have made has, against your purpose, grown disproportionate, one overswollen feature concealing all the rest, make the disproportion obvious to yourself by change of environment. Whether, having been made obvious, it can be altered is far from sure. Caricatures, once created, have a dismal habit of staying so, and a story containing as its main figure an unintended caricature is usually better abandoned than tinkered with. Ordinarily, the most you can hope to gain from experiments at betterment is a knowledge of what not to do another time.

Instances in which, meaning to present a character, you have instead feebly presented a personified trait, are less easy to discover. In the first draft of a story, there is no reason for your pausing to consider which you are committing to paper. As nearly as you can, you put down in that first draft whatever it is you want to say about your persons. But reading the draft over after it has cooled, or reading it aloud to a listener not committed in advance to approval, you find that what has reached the page is very far from being what you directed towards it. Whether trait or character, your main figure is ill-defined, incredible to the listener, uninteresting to him. The emotion he arouses is wavering or is too faint even to waver.

Changing the main figure to new surroundings, visualizing him inside your house or office gives little help. Those are transitions which can be accomplished by a person, by a personified trait, by a nonentity. What is most likely to be useful is an examination, as honest as you can make it, of your feeling towards your own creation. If it is a feeling all of one texture — all hate, all scorn, all mockery, even all unqualified admiration; if you

expect readers to feel as you do, would consider
your story a failure if they felt otherwise, then
probably what you are presenting is an isolated
trait. The feebleness of the presentation is likely to
spring from your having allowed yourself too broad
a base of observation. Try the story over, action after
action, speech after speech. Does any one of either
fail to give a reader's feeling some push towards
the desired end? Does any action, any speech, push
unintentionally in an opposite direction? Reread
"Good Wednesday", watching the sureness with
which the writer thrusts her victim towards complete denunciation. If you are presenting a trait, if
you are drawing a figure about which all readers
are to feel in one way and only one, then you can
afford no divergences. There your trait must stand,
undiminished by conflicting traits.

There is, however, a second and a more serious
reason for the failure of amateur stories setting forth
a personified trait. If you are placing a trait on
paper, are you sure, beyond all question, that the
trait itself — not your presentation of it but the raw
trait — is one which appears to other eyes as it does
to yours? Being sure of that, are you sure too that
the placing given your person does not too far
mitigate either his shortcoming or his virtue? Will
the embodiment of fault-finding you have created

seem to one reader mildly pathetic by reason of his age, to another justified because of enforced loneliness, and to both dull because their minds have failed to jump with yours?

Unaided, a writer rarely unearths in his own mind either of these possibilities. The trait, good or bad, which he is presenting seems to him unchangeably so. Since good is good and detestability is detestability, why should readers have differences of opinion about them?

A widened worldly experience is the best help here, but experience is slow to come by. If you have the habit of rigid classification, and still more if you entertain the set conviction that you do not have the habit, two steps towards improvement are open to you. One of these, of course, is an examination of how people around you, but outside your immediate family or group, feel towards characteristics which, to you, are faultless or irretrievably black. This examination, however, is valuable only after a suspicion has arisen in your mind that differences on the point in question are possible. An oblique fashion of discovering that they are is a return to the past. " 'Tis All For the Best", by Hannah More, displays a reduced gentlewoman whose repeated expression of meek trust is embodied in the title of the story.

Though Mrs. Simpson was the daughter of a clergyman and the widow of a genteel tradesman, she had been reduced, by a series of misfortunes, to accept a room in an almshouse. . . . One fine evening, as she was sitting reading her Bible . . . who should come and sit down by her but Mrs. Betty, who had formerly been lady's maid at the nobleman's house in the village of which Mrs. Simpson's father had been minister.

. . . But when Mrs. Simpson kindly addressed her as an old acquaintance, she screamed with surprise, "What you, madam? You in an almshouse, living on charity; you who used to be so charitable yourself . . ." "That may be one reason, Betty," replied Mrs. Simpson, "why Providence has provided this refuge for my old age. And my heart overflows with gratitude when I look back on His goodness." "No such great goodness," said Betty. "Why, you were born and bred a lady, and are now reduced to live in an almshouse." "Betty, I was born and bred a sinner, undeserving of the mercies I have received." "No such great mercies," said Betty. "Why, I heard that you had been turned out of doors; that your husband had broke; and that you had been in danger of starving.". . . "It is all true, Betty; glory be to God, it is all true." "Well," said Betty, "you are an odd sort of gentlewoman."

There is no question that Mrs. More admires her principal figure, presents her for admiration. Do you admire her? If not, why not? How do you feel

towards the main figures in Miss Edgeworth's
"Waste Not, Want Not"? Towards the heroine of
Washington Irving's "The Pride of the Village"?
Towards the young lady, embodiment of charity,
in "The Little Orange Sellers"? A careful look at
the presentation of traits once all white, once all
black, but now by no means so unspeckled, wakes
the mind to meditation on its own certitudes. These
are sometimes the certitudes of a single clique, a
single household, a small segment of country, their
power over others no greater than that of the
Widow Simpson over you. Turning your mind
around, if it is flexible enough to be turned, try
looking at your presented trait from the other
side. If you were not convinced in advance of its
rightness or wrongness, how would the person presented look to you then? Is there a chance that its
consistency in good or in evil is a consistency implausible to every one but you? In the twentieth
century, what are the traits inevitably to be ad-
mired, inevitably to be despised?

These, of course, are long-range questions. For
the story immediately in hand, once your suspicion
has been aroused about it, all you can do is to let
it lie by long enough after finishing to be sure
that your judgment is less partial than in the course
of writing, then to subject it to inquiry as critical

as you know how to make it. If you are part of a class, writing under guidance, differences of opinion within the group may help to dissolve your doubts, but in the last analysis you have to be your own critic.

Counsel given thus far is for avoiding or strengthening a caricature or a single-trait presentation. If what you are striving to put into words is a human being, fullsize and in the round, then whatever thing a book can do for you is found in chapters other than this one. The time required for your person's presentation can be considered, the point of observation most favorable to displaying him, the phrases for his characterization. But to capture understanding of the person himself is your own intimate struggle. Help there can be general only, not special.

IV

At the opening of the section just finished, it was noted that two general decisions about the persons to be presented in a story must be reached by a writer before his attention is turned to means of presentation. The second of these decisions relates not to how a writer is to characterize his figures but to whether it is necessary for him to characterize them at all. Are statue, bas-relief, caricature, any of them called for in the story he has in hand? Or is the function of the figure to be that of the peg on a cribbage board — something the player moves forward to show that the game has progressed?

Not all stories call for characterization. Not even all important and lasting stories do. There are those in which it is purposeless, those in which it is an intrusion, a detriment. The story which presents a puzzle for the reader's solving, the one devoted to analysis of an inevitable emotion, the allegory, the trick story — in each of these the total effect may well be reduced, not heightened, by the bringing alive of the figures concerned.

Illustration is drawn most readily from the detective story. Why is the reader willing to have the figures in the story knocked over like tenpins, a new one dead on the doorstep every time the door opens? The reason is that they are tenpins; the writer has made them so. Readers' enjoyment is decreased or destroyed if they are advanced to any more animated state. Detective stories containing careful characterization do exist, but the lasting ones, the exemplars, have little of it. So far as the detective himself is concerned, whether Dupin or Sherlock Holmes, he displays himself only as a collection of identifying mannerisms. The same mannerisms — of nonchalance, of reticence, of sudden revelation — serve for both, as they serve also for their important successors. As for the beings whom the detectives bring to justice, the beings they save from destruction, it is a fairly recent reader who can distinguish one from another unless by means of physical mark or external setting.

For a contemporary example, Dashiel Hammett's "Mr. Spade" will serve. Mr. Spade possesses nonchalance, possesses power of deduction. Bar these (which he shares with his more famous predecessors), he is any peg to be set in any hole. He is rightly so, for where sequence of happenings is of main importance, exactitudes of characterization make an unjustified demand on attention. In the original, not the derived, sense of the word, they are impertinent.

They are impertinent too in a story dealing with emotions so simplified as to be universal. In Poe's "Descent into a Maelstrom", the "I" who tells of the descent has white hair, has been a fisherman, is now broken. This much the reader is told, but this goes no farther in characterization than would a man's having been a grocery clerk, retired because of rheumatism. The figure shown is representative only. It is humanity itself, not some identified particle from the mass, which makes that unparalleled descent. In the greater number of *Tales of Horror,* the same thing is true of the "I" who acts as teller. It is true of the "I" or the "he" in thousands of ghost stories. The conditions set forth in them are conditions by which every human being would be affected as is the hero. The hero is Everyman; there is no point in distinguishing him farther.

There is no point, either, in distinguishing the figures in an allegory, for here it is not even Everyman with whom the story is concerned but merely one particular thread pulled from the general human stuff. Mr. Worldly Wiseman is worldly wise — no more. He is a "character" only in the special sense of the word. To see this kind of "character" in its perfection and to see too from what the personified trait draws its being, a reader can do no better than to turn back to collections put together in the seventeenth century, when the "Seventeenth-Century Character" was plentiful enough to gain a special designation.

The Obstinate Man does not hold opinions, but they hold him; for when he is once possest with an error, 'tis like the Devil, not to be cast out but with great difficulty. Whatsoever he lays hold on, like a drowning man, he never loses though it do but help to sink him the sooner. . . . The slighter and more inconsistent his Opinions are, the faster he holds them, otherwise they would fall asunder of themselves; for opinions that are false ought to be held with more Strictness and Assurance than those that are true, or they will betray their Owners before they are aware.

An Hypocrite is a Saint that goes by clockwork, a Machine made by the Devil's Geometry, which he winds and nicks to go as he pleases. He is the Devil's Finger-Watch, that never goes true but too fast or too slow as he sets him.

Earle, Hall, Overbury, Butler — any one of them is a mine of information and of short-story suggestions to the writers of a later century.

The trick story is, in one particular, like the detective story — the more emphasis on trick, the less on characterization. And even more than with the detective story, it is wise here for a beginner to make sure that his own mind is clear as to the difference between characterizing a figure and assigning to it certain identifying marks. Identifications have been accumulated for most of the set figures in fiction. When Frank Stockton describes the father in "The Lady or the Tiger", ". . . a semi-barbaric king . . . a man of exuberant fancy, and, withal, of an authority so irresistible that, at his will, he turned his varied fancies into facts", he is obviously not directing his description to the purpose of making his subject come alive for the reader. He is assigning to him the customary stock-in-trade of oriental tyrants in order that he may be ready for use in the plot. To bring father or princess or lover into existence would be to ruin the story; they have to remain subordinated to the trick. But when, in "The Real Thing", Henry James characterizes Major and Mrs. Monarch, "It was in their faces, the blankness, the deep intellectual repose of the twenty years of country-house visiting which had given them their pleasant intonations", he is referring them to their type, but he is by no means presenting them with stock characteristics.

These two stories are familiar, at least by hearsay, to most readers. Rereading of them, attention centered on the persons shown, will probably provide all the understanding needed concerning subordination of character in the trick story. For his own work, the writer of a trick story need only ask himself what within the story would be changed if his persons were filled out into human beings instead of being left with merely identifying characteristics? If anything would, would that change enhance the value of the trick or detract from it?

To decide how far characterization should go in a story predominantly concerned with action is less easy. Study of two or three stories from a magazine devoted to "Westerns" in contrast with two or three from, say, some volume of Joseph Conrad's is useful here. In most of the "Western" stories, it will be found that the hero is limited to those stock characteristics which are all he needs for rescue of the heroine or defeat of the bandits. When his spiritual state, his fears, his self-questionings, his agony of indecision before the first shot is fired — when these become important, then the story, no matter how much action it holds, is no longer a story of action. Conrad's *Lord Jim* contains battle, murder, and sudden death in abundance; with Lord Jim's soul taken out, there would still be material left for an excellent adventure story. With the soul in, it is the story of that soul — no boy's book, for all its high excitements and tropic splendors.

The writer who has written a story pressed full of action, and who, looking back over it, finds it wavering between two aims, has first of all to make up his mind. Does he wish chiefly to forward the action? Or does he wish to illuminate a soul? In the one instance, he is writing a boy's story, even though the boy he aims at may have been a boy for his full seventy years. In the other, he is interpreting a human being. One or the other must predominate. If action is to be important for itself, then the actor needs those qualities, and only those, which fit him for his performance. To give him more is to make him as ineffective as a fireman who stops to explain his mental attitude towards fires in front of a conflagration.

V

So far, discussion of character has proceeded as though character stood by itself in a story. It does not in stories any more than it does in life. It never does. It stands always in relation to circumstance.

Leaving out of account the stories where character has no importance or only the slightest, we find that the relations between the person and the set of happenings in which he is enmeshed are, as might be foreseen, identical with those which in life exist between the human being and his circumstances. Each given its separate paragraph, the relations are these:

The person may remain unaltered by circumstance.

The person and the circumstances surrounding him may each affect the other, but with the person directing the course which circumstance shall take.

The person may seem to have mastered circumstance but be outwitted by it in the end.

The person may be molded by conditions he can in no way change.

The person may be the passive recipient of happenings, tossed about by them but making no convincing effort against them.

The five relations have this in common — that in each the individual is the center of importance. Happenings matter or do not matter as they affect him or as they show the impossibility of his being affected. In much the greater number of stories, the persons presented fall within the second and third groups. Let us dispose first, then, of the three less usual presentations.

In the first relationship, the person is unchanged by circumstance. Of what kind of person can this be predicated? What variety of human walks through life, as Shadrach through the furnace, neither putting out the flames nor scorched by them?

One example is the main figure in Conrad Aiken's "Silent Snow, Secret Snow", the story of a child mind which slowly withdraws itself from the external. No alteration in the pathetic boy hero of the story is due to circumstance. Neither happenings at school nor at home, neither the presence of affection nor the pressures of family anxiety halt the march of his obsession. From beginning to end, he is altered only as alteration takes place from within — as he, or whatever secret force is at work on him, directs it. Circumstances are no more than the frame around the picture. The increase of his obsession has nothing to do with father, mother, doctor, teacher. His own special daemon, and that only, is in control. When he breaks from doctor and parents to run to his own room; when, addressing his mother, the words "tore themselves from his other life suddenly, 'Mother! Mother! Go away! I hate you!'" it is for no fault of his mother's, it is in answer to no outside event. He recognizes no exterior circumstance, only the urge of his own inner necessity.

Stories of disordered minds, many stream-of-consciousness stories, some dealing with the personified trait, are of this kind. Stories where an ordinary figure — not mad, not completely egoist, not shown only from beneath the shield of his own consciousness — is presented as invulnerable, are fairly sure to be based on a single extraordinary happening or on a final reversal of expectation. Two of Stacy Ammonier's stories, "Miss Bracegirdle Does Her Duty" and "The Great Unimpressionable", are representatives of the two kinds. Miss Bracegirdle, impeccable spinster sister of an English curate, spends the night under the bed of a dead desperado in a strange Paris hotel. She emerges from the ordeal a little disheveled perhaps, a little discomfited, but exactly the same Miss Bracegirdle still, with no mark of experience on her. There is, in reality, no reason why a mark should be on her. She has slipped into grotesque and dangerous circumstances as she might have slipped into a puddle. She slips out from them, takes her routine morning bath, and the mud is gone. "The Great Unimpressionable" shows an English villager going through the war. The events of the war, which he can neither alter nor comprehend, leave him untouched; the death of his dog does not. He is, therefore, not a figure untouched by circumstance but, like all of us, one touched only by those circumstances which come within his comprehension.

Stories showing the person molded by circumstances he cannot change have been frequent in the last decade. An example as enlightening in its presentation of minor figures as of the major one is Tess Slesinger's "Jobs in the Sky." Here major and minor figures alike are hypnotized by the rush of pre-Christmas selling in a great store. Joey Andrews, laboring joyously, half intoxicated by the mere chance to labor — "recollections of his eight months' nightmare among the unhired was unworthy of No. 19–23, 167B of a great department store" — is discharged from that store at the end of the day, the Christmas rush being over. Against his will, in spite of his utmost effort, the impersonal machinery of the store thrusts him back to tramphood. The machinery itself turns on, unchanged by his coming, his going. An older example of the same molding process, and a less desolate one, is found in Edward Everett Hale's familiar story, "The Man Without a Country", the incidents of which almost any reader can review in his own mind.

Stories where the person is submerged by circumstance differ from those just quoted only in that struggle, if it ever existed, has ceased before the story opens. Any story of a typical hour is necessarily the story of a person submerged, whether with his own initial consent or against it. Unless he has been submerged, reduced to predicable action, and the reader knows him to be so reduced, the hours or days chosen for presentation cannot be made to seem typical. "Not Wanted", by Anton Chekhov, is an example which makes clear the difference between person molded and person passively enduring. Throughout the story, its main figure, a middle-class Russian, is continually irritated by the conditions of his life. He complains at them, he despises them, he lifts no finger to change them. Covering only the length of some ten hours, the story both shows those hours and overwhelmingly compels the reader to believe that all other hours, wherever placed, will be, in emotional effect, precisely like them. The main figure is alive but alive only to be annoyed at his fate, not to struggle against it. Something of the same effect of recurrence is produced by Conrad Aiken's "The Dark City." Its opening sentence, "His greatest pleasure in life came always at dusk", proclaims the repetitive nature of the story's happenings.

But thus far most Americans appear to see life as a struggle between man and circumstance in which man has not yet surrendered. Most writers therefore so depict it. The victory may lie on the one side or on the other, but neither man nor circumstance fails of being altered. The figure is in control when he is shown as directing happenings by his own responses to them, not impervious to what goes on outside him but yet the master of his essential self. Circumstance wins only when that essential self is overpowered.

An example or two from life makes clear the pattern fiction follows here. History can furnish them in plenty. Observation can furnish them. Sir Thomas More, jesting in his prison and on his way to death — "But say you, being higher up, am I not nearer to heaven in this prison than in mine own house?" . . . "Have a care for me going up to the scaffold,

Master Lieutenant. I can shift for myself coming down" — is wholly master of circumstance. He dies, but he does so because of happenings which his own decision has brought into being. At the other end of the scale — and still from history — Northumberland, whose attempt at treason has ended in failure, gives happenings their start indeed, but once the start is given, he is tossed about by them, his essential self reduced to an ineffectual gelatinous quivering. In any reader's own neighborhood, in his own family, either figure may be matched. Matching them, deciding on them, is one of those many parts of the business of writing which is never finished. The unceasing evaluation and re-evaluation of human beings in relation to their environment goes on throughout all a writer's life.

"May Day Celebration", by T. O. Beachcroft, provides a fictional example to supplement the historical ones just given. The person here, an English labor agitator, selfless, fanatic, has indeed been altered by circumstance — ". . . his face, once full of fire and expression, had grown dour and set and stubborn" — but throughout the story he has himself caused circumstances to be what they are. They have shaped him, but they have been given the chance to do so only at his own will. Had that will altered, circumstances must have been altered in response to the change. However malignant towards him, they are still his servants.

The wife, from whose point of observation the story is told, has also been in constant struggle, wins also a final though qualified triumph. The husband having been arrested, she remains alone in the flat.

The door closed; and she was alone.

She stood silent for a long time, thinking and seeing nothing.

Then she slowly walked to the window and pulled the curtains. How grimy they were! She sat down beside the table, which still carried the remains of tea. Many pictures of her broken and tattered life passed before her. She saw her hopes of the future torn in ragged dirty pieces, fluttering away. She knew now that she would never have a home; that from now on she need never hope for a home. The pictures of the little house she had begun to see changed to pictures of rooms in worse and worse streets; to fierce poverty, bare boards, and fireless grates, to comfortless old age.

Yet she felt calm and almost joyful. She had seen the look in Thomas's eyes. She knew he was living through the proudest and happiest moments of his whole life. She fell to thinking of the red and white cheeks, the wild black hair, he used to have. And gradually her heart grew light.*

* From *You Must Break Out Sometimes*, by T. O. Beachcroft. Published by Harper and Brothers, New York

It is evident that freedom of choice, freedom of will, is left with the persons in the story. It is a limited freedom — "that child's plaything, a drop of water in a globe of glass" — but freedom it is none the less. The main impulsions come from within.

The stories everybody has read, "The Minister's Black Veil", "The Courting of Dinah Shadd", "The Man Who Corrupted Hadleyburg", "The End of the Tether", even a piece of folklore so intentionally fantastic as "The Devil and Daniel Webster" — all of these belong in this category. Once the story is under way, character directs circumstance. Happenings must stop dead or change their course if character be altered, for the happenings continue to exist only because of the kind of person on whom they act.

The person who seems to have mastered circumstance but has not, or seems to be its victim but turns out surprisingly to be its master is, of course, found oftenest in the surprise-ending story. He has usually been prepared for there by a full set of implications — signposts which the reader might decipher if only he would. Wilbur Daniel Steele's "The Man Who Saw Through Heaven" is an example of the conquered finally conquering. The main figure, a missionary, just married and on his way to his first foreign charge, chances before sailing to visit an astronomical laboratory, peer for the first time through the lens of a powerful telescope. The glimpse sends crashing his conception of an arranged universe, of a personal God looking from a placed Heaven straight at him. Halfway across the ocean, he goes technically "mad", escapes at a port of call, and wanders desolate through Africa, seeking the God he has lost, making mud idols to represent him. When those who track him find the spot where he is buried, they find too the last idol, the rediscovered God.

The figure was crudeness itself, but . . . an attitude of interest . . . intense and static, breathless and eternal . . . penetrating to its bottom atom, to the last electron, to a hill upon it, and to a two-legged mite about to die. Marking (yes, I'll swear to the incredible) the sparrow's fall.*

Treatments of the main figure which allow him direction of circumstances throughout the story or final victory over them call usually for an attitude on the part of the writer respectful to the human beings with whom he deals. Satire, mockery, the whole set of belittling attitudes, have implicit in

* From "The Man Who Saw Through Heaven." By permission of Wilbur Daniel Steele

them the power of circumstance to thwart human intent. In stories ironic, satiric, or humorous, then, we find reversals that leave the person who apparently has been successful gasping at the end under the shock of unforeseen failure. Which kind of stories a writer produces depends usually less on his immediate will than on his inner, and often unrecognized, convictions. For in dealing with character, he can in the main deal with it only as he believes it to be. To read in close succession a dozen stories by one writer, attention set while reading on the relation between the main figure and the circumstances surrounding him, is to get full proof of how here even more than elsewhere in writing, a writer consistently sets down his own deep-buried convictions.

VI

To learn to put character on the page with even partial success is a task to fill most of a writer's years. It is infant-class work, however, in comparison with the task always preceding and always accompanying it — that of trying to comprehend character. Lack of writing skill may make a comprehended character stalk woodenly through the pages; lack of comprehension makes that woodenness unavoidable. How, then, is a beginner at writing to increase his knowledge of why some certain being reacts in a given fashion to given happenings?

All the earlier part of his learning will be unconscious. Fra Lippo Lippi explains one method, traditionally effective.

> . . . when a boy starves in the streets
> Eight years together, as my fortune was,
> Watching folks' faces to know who will fling
> The bit of half-stripped grape-bunch he desires,
> And who will kick and curse him for his pains . . .
> Why, sense and soul of him grow sharp alike,
> He learns the look of things . . .

Learning the look of things through a life lived actually — not by way of slumming parties — on the edge of annihilation has sharpened the soul and sense of perhaps a third as many potential writers as it has destroyed. Another method of sharpening is to have grown up in a large and vocal household, one where actions and motives come into lively review. Still another is to have struggled as a child through prolonged illnesses till, reading being a sole recourse, book people became real, and the analyses of their actions carried over into life.

When childhood is once past, though, these opportunities are past too. For an adult, there are left only three means capable of a practice directed by the will.

One of these is the determined beating down of self-consciousness. It is difficult to get understanding of other people if you are constantly concerned with what they may be thinking of you. A blanket of self-consciousness wrapped round you is as muffling to your senses as would be an actual blanket.

A second means is the cultivating of that listening habit discussed under *Dialogue* but worth cultivation for much more than the use suggested there. Whole-hearted listening is impossible when most of your attention is centered on what you yourself will presently say in answer. The invaluable capacity to submerge yourself in some one else's experience, in some one else's speculation or emotion, is a capacity which can be cultivated — if not perfectly, yet to a considerable degree. Some fiction writers, it is true, have been afflicted with that "desire to shine" which Boswell imputes to Goldsmith, some have been inordinate talkers. But in spite of exceptions, listening, undisturbed absorption in the scene presented, is all but a necessity for the writer whose later business will be with realistic fiction. Somewhere in his voluminous self-depictions, H. G. Wells has pointed out that one of his chief blessings was his

having been a young man of insignificant presence
and reedy voice. Whether he would or would not, he
was continually overlooked. Having resigned himself to being overlooked, he had his whole attention
to give to others, a kind of invisible recording instrument at the lower end of the dinner table.

The third means for developing an understanding
of character is more definite — again, an exercise
for those odd-minute considerations without which
practice of fiction comes to nothing. Pick up the
news weekly in the dentist's office and turn to
Personals.

Mr. and Mrs. John Hagen departed this week on their
second honeymoon. Mr. Hagen, fifty-five, and his wife,
fifty-three, were first married in 1905, were divorced in
1907 after the birth of their only child, and yesterday
were remarried at their son's home. Mr. Hagen is well
known as the manager . . .

You can stop there. You will never write a story
about the Hagen family. You do not want to write
a story about them, and yet — why did they do it?
Why did she? There are plots enough to snap into
mind along with the situation, but plots just now are
not of the essence of the matter. Emotions are.
What did she feel as she stood there, middle-aged,
bordering on old, marrying the man from whom she

had been divorced for a generation? What had life done to her in that generation to make her willing to tolerate what once had been intolerable? Is it in the phrase, "at their son's home" that the secret lies? You begin to think of her so — a woman absorbed in a small child, a woman wrapping her smothering affection around a growing boy, a woman displaced now by her son's wife. Is it her importunate need of being needed which pushes her into marriage? If it is, how does she feel as the cadenced phrases of the marriage service sound in her ear? Whom have you known like her — what woman whose need of being needed, of preparing surprise desserts and being praised for them, of hunting out rubbers on rainy days and straw hats on sunny ones, of shaping her life around a home-coming hour, is stronger in her than any inner resource? While Mrs. Hagen is still inhabiting your mind, read Chekhov's "The Darling." Is Mrs. Hagen that?

There are a dozen other things she may be, but no one of them is useful to you merely as a chance thought. It has to be a thought pursued, a thought blossoming out into mental images and stirred emotions before it becomes a help to understanding character.

An allied mental activity, also an odd-minute one, gives aid both to understanding and presentation.

The thoroughly commonplace man sitting across the aisle from you on this early morning commuters' train — how does he differ from the commonplace man one seat farther on? Scribbling in your notebook, you try one sentence for him, you try another. You try to get at him directly by description, obliquely by attribution of characteristics, obliquely still by comparisons or contrasts.

Learning to characterize, that is, is a full-time occupation. When you are not brooding over the figures in your own story, you are noticing, wondering, interpreting. Power of characterization comes, most of it, not through conscious, time-set practice but through an attitude of mind compounded in almost equal parts of curiosity, of emotional responsiveness, of habit of meditation. It cannot be created by will power, but if it exists at all it can be increased, as any other innate capacity is increased, by the intelligent application of will to the end sought.

VIII

DIALOGUE

. . . any one of us recognizes clearly that he may know all the rules of the grammar of a foreign language, may speak the language with the correct pronunciation; but until he acquires something that is the characterizing "chant", lilt, cadence of that language, he never speaks it like a native. What distinguishes us as we come from different parts of this country is not so much the rolled *r* of the Middle Westerner or the prolonged New England *a*; it is this same rhythm and cadence of speech.

Suggested Reading

BRADFORD, ROARK. "Child of God." *Harper's Magazine,* April, 1927

BRADSHAW, GEORGE. "No." *Saturday Evening Post,* October 13, 1934

DAY, PRICE. "22." *Saturday Evening Post,* October 16, 1937

DERLETH, AUGUST W. "The Old Lady Has Her Day." *Scribner's Magazine,* July, 1936

FREEMAN, R. AUSTIN. "The Case of Oscar Brodski." *The Singing Bone.* New York, Dodd, Mead and Company

HEMINGWAY, ERNEST. "The Killers." *Men Without Women.* New York, Charles Scribner's Sons

HOUGH, DONALD. "Hold It, Please." *Saturday Evening Post,* September 11, 1937

LARDNER, RING. "The Love Nest." *Roundup and Other Stories.* New York, Charles Scribner's Sons

STEINBECK, JOHN. "The Raid." *North American Review,* October, 1934

THIELEN, BENEDICT. "I Believe." *Harper's Magazine,* August, 1937

WALPOLE, HUGH. "Mother's a Pity." *Collier's,* January 8, 1938

Dialogue

"The trouble with my stories is that I can't seem to think up anything to write about and I can't make my people talk."

THE woman whose analysis of her difficulties is quoted above was perhaps a woman meant for some profession other than writing. She is, however, in her second admission naming a difficulty by no means only hers. To cause people to talk in a story is not merely to make them speak; it is also to provide for their forwarding the story by their talking, for their expressing something of their own characters, for their fitting the tone of their talk to the tone of the whole.

Written sentences are almost never a transcript of spoken ones, and this in spite of the fact that a first step in the writing of dialogue is to learn to listen. After listening comes the prolonged process — usually the conscious process — of changing the written speech from the form in which it actually was spoken to the form which makes it sound to readers as though it had been spoken, and at the same time of making it perform its required work in the story.

Now and then a writer arrives in whom the ability to listen is innate. Where it is not, it is fortunately one which can be cultivated, and cultivation, once the need for it is recognized, can go on indefinitely. First, though, the need must be recognized — the exact kind of need. For listening, so far as the writer is concerned, is not a matter of getting the sense of what is said. It is a matter of getting the swing, the time, the individual marks of individual talk.

Except for geniuses and mimics, listeners hear usually only the substance of conversation. Even strongly marked differences between speaker and speaker are rarely heard with enough acuteness to allow for reproduction. Try writing down, without reference to books, a paragraph as spoken by some person with a foreign accent, and discover how little except the sense of the speech and perhaps an occasional striking phrase sticks in your mind. The national or racial or personal idiosyncrasies represented in your paragraph are far more likely to be idiosyncrasies learned from reading than from actual hearing. If you try to write three or four sentences as spoken by some member of your family, you will again discover that your habit in listening is to grasp the meaning of what the speaker says and to disregard his way of saying it. Probably you will never exactly copy either the dialect of a given racial group or those lesser peculiarities which, within a group, set off one member from another. None the less, listening — listening for the tone, the tune of talk — provides the only base on which dialogue may be built.

After listening, comes transcription. The Boswellian retirement to a corner to set down sentences still hot from the tongue is practicable only for a Boswell. But there are opportunities — on trains, in 'bus stations, in the family living-room — first for listening, then for the immediate exact recording of successive sentences informally spoken. These are opportunities to be used not once but again and again, for transcription and more transcription and still more, even of the veriest scraps of talk, is valuable as a preliminary to writing. No untrained person can trust his recollection to preserve the word arrangement, the accent, the diction of a speaker — not, at least, to preserve them accurately enough for later study. It is true that the sentences transcribed will not be used in the story a writer is immediately at work on or in any later story, but the value of what is set down does not lie in its being itself story material. It lies in its teaching the transcriber something about the way sentences actually are spoken, something too about the changes necessary for transforming spoken dialogue into written.

Of these changes, the first is compression. Talk exactly recorded is talk redundant to the point of absurdity. It blocks the story, it leaves no space for anything but talk. Sinclair Lewis has an especial talent for the writing of dialogue which gives the effect of falling from the speaker's lips, unconsidered, loose, full. Yet comparison of any passage he has written with the conversation of persons such as those displayed shows how cunningly he makes one word do the work of three, one sentence the work of a dozen.

"Just been making a trip through the South. Business conditions not very good down there," said one of the council.

"Is that a fact? Not very good, eh?"

"No, didn't strike me they were up to normal."

"Not up to normal, eh?"

"No, I wouldn't hardly say they were."

The whole council nodded sagely and decided, "Yump, not hardly up to snuff."

"Well, business conditions ain't what they ought to be out West neither, not by a long shot."

"That's a fact. And I guess the hotel business feels it. That's one good thing, though; these hotels that've been

charging five bucks a day — yes, and maybe six-seven —
for a rotten room are going to be darn glad to get four,
and maybe give you a little service."

"That's a fact. Say, uh, speaking about hotels, I hit
the St. Francis at San Francisco for the first time the
other day, and, say, it certainly is a first-class place."

"You're right, brother! The St. Francis is a swell place
— absolutely A–1."

"That's a fact. I'm right with you. It's a first-class
place." *

The loquacity of the group, the repetitiousness,
the tiresomeness are achingly evident. The sense of
the talk's going on interminably, folding and re-
folding itself about the same unimportant topics, is
fully conveyed. And yet the reading time is of the
briefest. How the effect is created, how much of it
comes from subject matter and how much from
wording, is worth any beginner's study. It is worth
it not only in the passage given but still more in those
conversations he seeks out and sets down for himself and later tries to reduce, without loss of effect,
from three pages to one.

Compression, however, is only the first of the
needed changes. Observe the following question and
answer, taken down exactly from the lips of two
speakers unconscious of audience.

* From *Babbitt*, by Sinclair Lewis. Copyright, 1922, by Harcourt,
Brace and Company, Inc.

"Who's t' go? Got 'ny idea?"

"I do' know. No' un fr' here s' far as I've heard. O'course, meeting in Bahs'n . . ."

Illiterates? No, philologists discussing a prospective meeting of the Modern Language Association. In casual conversation, all speakers slur vowels, drop final consonants, take short cuts through syntax. The result is that, so far as the reader is concerned, speech put on the page as it falls from the lips of the speaker sends that speaker sliding precipitously down the social scale. Not only does what he says require trimming to fit the space allotted to it, it has also to be dressed out with those final "g's" and central "t's" which every tongue neglects. If exact transcription had no other value, it would still be worth while for pointing out the effect of unaltered reproduction on an imaginary person's social standing.

Even the writing of dialect is never actually a reproduction. It is moderated in behalf of the reader, who is willing to pay just so much toll and no more for the privilege of being introduced to strange scenes and persons. Observe the passage following, one taken from "Gentlemen of the Party", by G. Street Dutton.

"I 'low wold Nick spiled the shape o' they downs, Jargie, ut o' cussedness, zno. 'Appen th' Almighty made

'em strightish an' then the devil, 'ee come along an' bit
out a chunk yer an' there fur 'is dinner. Cum up, vi'let.
When we gits awver right thic next 'ump, we'll be nigh
'ome an' stable."

Too much to pay for what is gained? For many
readers it would be.

In "Child of God", by Roark Bradford, Willie, the
childlike colored hero, makes a much smaller demand.

"Cap'm Archie say he gonter bring me a ten-cent
cigar to go walkin' up de gallows wid in my mouf'. . . .
An' I makes me a speech up yonder — "

The marks of a negro speaker are on the sentences,
but no word is even momentarily unintelligible.

Elsie Singmaster, with her Pennsylvania Dutch,
is still more sparing, using inversions and an occasional oddity of phrase, but keeping well within the
limits of easy comprehension. Dialect on the page,
as contrasted with dialect on the tongue, accomplishes its end by suggestion of difference rather than
by presentation of it.

By strict interpretation, every human who speaks,
speaks dialect. No one is free from racial and local
speech marks, whether the "different to" of the
Englishman as against the "different from" of the
American, or the forthright r's of the Rockies in

contrast with the absentee r's of Virginia. For a writer, however, the problem is only what special marks and how many or few of them must be put on paper for the sake of characterization, or for differentiating one person or group from the rest. Every mark is paid for by a fragment of extra effort on the reader's part. Unless it accomplishes a purpose, it is not worth paying for. And with dialect as with the speech which falls short of dialect, what the individual would actually have said has to be lightened, corrected, rearranged to bring it from mouth to page without exaggeration of its special quality. Witness the two boys talking in the following paragraph:

"H'ya, Butch," said Roddy.

"H'ya, Roddy."

"What you doing?"

"I'm building a boat a trillion miles long. What does it look like I'm doing?"

Roddy sat down on the grass and watched. "Want to make a buck?" he said.

"Sure!" Then suspiciously, "How?"

"Oh, old Jean What's-Her-Name's going to have a party in that barn on their farm, and she wants the barn cleaned up first, some reason or other."

"Her!"

"Yeh. But a buck's a buck."

"A buck!"

"Well, if she's crazy enough to pay it, I'll take it."

"Me, too!"

"It's not our fault if she ought to have her head examined, I guess."

— Price Day, "22" *

The manner of the imaginary person's speech shows his social position, his temperament or character, his race or his nationality. Along with any or all of these, however, it must also advance the story. Observe the uses of the three conversations which follow:

"Mr. Claridge," Hewitt proceeded slowly, "when did you first find that Lord Stanway's cameo was a forgery?"

Claridge literally bounced in his chair. His face paled but he managed to stammer sharply, "What — what — what d'you mean? Forgery? Do you mean to say I sell forgeries? Forgery? It wasn't a forgery!"

"Then," continued Hewitt, "if it wasn't a forgery, why did you destroy it and burst your trap door and desk to imitate a burglary?" . . .

"Destroy it? What — what — I didn't — didn't destroy it!"

"Threw it in the river, then — don't prevaricate about details."

— Arthur Morrison, "The Stanway Cameo Mystery" †

* In the *Saturday Evening Post,* October 16, 1937
† From *Martin Hewitt Investigates,* by Arthur Morrison

Last time he had come to see her, Basil had worn a rose in his buttonhole. How handsome he had looked in that bright blue suit, with that dark red rose! . . .

"The headmaster's wife keeps asking me to dinner. It's a perfect nuisance. I never get an evening to myself in that place."

"But can't you refuse?"

"Oh, well, it doesn't do for a man in my position to be unpopular."

— Katherine Mansfield, "The Singing Lesson" *

. . . one evening there was a little scene. Laura suddenly snapped out:

"Please don't keep looking at me, Mother." And Mrs. Kinghorn, with a frightened, startled expression, said:

"I'm not looking at you, darling, I'm reading my book."

"Oh, no, you're not. You are watching me all the time."

"Watching you, dearie? What should I be watching you for? I'll go upstairs if you'd rather."

"Oh, no, of course not. I'm going out soon."

Then Mrs. Kinghorn said quietly, "It's quite natural."

"What is?" asked Laura.

"That I should irritate you both. Don't think I don't understand."

"There's nothing to understand," Laura cried, exasperated to madness, jumping to her feet. "Only we can't

* From *The Garden Party*, by Katherine Mansfield. By permission of Alfred A. Knopf, publisher

escape you, John and I. It's a dreadful feeling that somebody is watching you every minute of the day and night."

"Don't I know it?" said Mrs. Kinghorn cheerfully. "It was just the same with me when I was engaged to Richard. Richard's mother meant well, and I mean well, but until you're married, you'll find me tiresome. The sooner you're married, the better."

"What are you going to do then?" asked Laura.

"Oh, I'll be all right. Don't worry about me." She pushed her skinny hand through her short sunset hair. "Don't worry about me, darling. I'll be quite all right in some little place by myself."

Laura, in a perfect passion, answered, "Oh, why will you be so good and so self-sacrificing? Why don't you say something mean or spiteful?"

Mrs. Kinghorn answered placidly, "I dare say I could be mean and spiteful if I tried. Most women can," and went on with her book.

— Hugh Walpole, "Mother's a Pity" *

In the first excerpt, taken from a detective story, what we get from dialogue is fact, evidence accumulated by one person and explained for the reader's benefit to another.

In the second, the speech of Basil is the writer's device for injuring him in the reader's eyes. It is

* In *Collier's Magazine*, January 8, 1938. Used by permission of Eric S. Pinker and Adrienne Morrison, Inc., author's agents

out of his own mouth that he is convicted, and that by no more than a single sentence.

So, though for the opposite purpose, speech is used in "Mother's a Pity." Here, though, neither mother nor daughter is sacrificed, yet the character of each, the relation between them, a forecast of the action of the story, are all implicit in a dialogue which, so far as concerns the words actually said, reveals only a thwarted attempt at a quarrel.

The dialogues given thus far have been from realistic stories, the writers forming the speeches of their persons to sound in the reader's ears like actual speech. Things said and way of saying have alike been directed towards producing an illusion of reality. Few readers need to be reminded that the illusion of reality is not always the illusion sought. Wodehouse, Dunsany, Cabell — a host of others — emphasize the point. "People do not talk that way" is an accusation which has standing against the realistic story only. The chance critics to whom a beginner at writing is exposed use the assertion often as though it were a universal condemnation. It is not. Beyond being intelligible, dialogue need have nothing to do with actuality. What it does have to do with is the especial atmosphere in which the story is set. In "Jeeves and the Unbidden Guest", Bertie Wooster, in his capacity of unwilling host, goes with

Jeeves to the front door to find his visitor lying on
the mat.

"He's had some sort of dashed fit," I said. I took an-
other look. "Jeeves! Someone's been feeding him meat!"
"Sir?"
"He's a vegetarian, you know. He must have been dig-
ging into a planked steak or something. Call up a doc-
tor!"
"I hardly think it will be necessary, sir. If you would
take his lordship's legs, while I—"
"Great Scott, Jeeves! You don't think—he can't
be—"
"I'm inclined to think so, sir."
And by Jove, he was right. Once on the right track,
you couldn't mistake it. Motty was under the surface.
It was the deuce of a shock.
"You never can tell, Jeeves!"
"Very seldom, sir."
"Remove the eye of authority and where are you?"
"Precisely, sir."
"Where is my wandering boy tonight and all that
sort of thing, what!"
"It would seem so, sir."
"Well, we had better bring him in, eh?"
"Yes, sir."

.   .   .   .

Next morning . . . I went to Motty's room to investi-
gate . . .

"What ho!" I said.

"What ho!" said Motty.

"What ho! What ho!"

"What ho! What ho! What ho!" *

Nobody believes or is expected to believe that Bertie or Jeeves or Motty or any other human beings would actually talk in the fashion given. But the glittering absurdity, the breathless circus-ring mirthfulness of the story, is strengthened by it. So with many of the exchanges of speech in Mark Twain's "The Man Who Corrupted Hadleyburg." So, to an end quite different, the rolling periods in Cabell's early stories.

Then these three princes rose and knelt before the priest; they were clad in long bright garments, and they glittered with gold and many jewels. He standing among them shuddered in his sombre robe. "Hail, King of England!" cried these three.

"Hail, ye that are my kinsmen!" he answered; "hail, ye that spring of an accursed race, as I! And woe to England for that hour wherein Manuel of Poictesme held traffic with the Sorceress of Provence, and the devil's son begot an heir for England! Of ice and of lust and of hell-fire are all we sprung; and old records attest it; and fickle and cold and ravenous and without shame are all

* From *Carry On, Jeeves*, by P. G. Wodehouse, copyright, 1916, reprinted by permission from Doubleday, Doran and Company, Inc.

our race until the end. Of our brother's dishonor ye make merchandise today, and today fratricide whispers me, and leers, and Heaven help me! I attend."

— James Branch Cabell, "The Satraps"*

The conviction that dialogue is conversation transferred to paper is one to get rid of early. "That is the way they did talk" is no more an excuse for pointless printed speech than "That is what did happen" is an excuse for implausible action. Talk, like action, must fit to the setting, the tune, of the story.

But the fact that it must fit having been first grasped and later enforced by reading and observation, what are you, a beginner at writing, to do next to improve the dialogue in your own stories? Means of general improvement have already been named. You are to listen and to continue to listen. You are to write down conversation exactly and then to rework what you have written until, having ceased to be the thing you heard, it has come instead to appear upon the page as though it were that thing. These two processes are for the good of all your future writing. For the story you have in hand at the moment, all that you can do is to isolate and interrogate the dialogue passages. What do you want a particular piece of dialogue to do? Is it to carry

*By permission of Robert M. McBride and Company, publishers

information, elucidate character, enhance the story's mood? Does it have the right sound when read aloud? Is its tone and tune and diction similar to those of other passages by the same speaker? Finally, is it worth the space it takes? Nowhere is a story more likely to spill itself without purpose across the page than in its dialogue. Nowhere does it more readily exhibit inconsistencies.

"I ain't going," said Julia. "Well, that's enough for you, ain't it? I tell yuh I don't want to go.". . .

.   .   .   .

"Why should I?" Julia asked, looking away from him. "You didn't want me. You wanted her. You asked me only because you thought you had to."

In the story from which the two passages just quoted are taken, three pages separate them, but three pages are not enough, all the pages in the story are not enough, to allow for Julia's transformation. That transformation is not the result of her saying "ain't" on one page and avoiding it on another or yet the "yuh" which makes its appearance in the third sentence. The essential difference is in the ring of the sentences. Consistency can come only from the writer's realizing the presented person, being conscious of shock when a speaker steps out of one character into another.

As in many other places, acting out a scene will sometimes help. When you speak his words aloud, does the person on page one sound on page five like the same person? Do his sentences, as you pronounce them, have likenesses in syntax, in accent, in diction, which mark them as his? Placed in the situation and addressing the listener that has been provided for him, would the speaker speak as he does? In the same rounded sentences, in the same full paragraphs? Or does his maker know, so soon as he reads the paragraphs aloud, that no listener would passively receive those solid ammunition rounds of information or opinion? No dialogue, spoken or written, is made up exclusively of words. Watch the unspoken interruptions which break in on even the most solid blocks of talk. One speaker may speak steadily for minutes. None the less, his speech is continually interrupted. He turns, gesticulates, hesitates. His listener, saying nothing, evinces agreement, boredom, anger. In actual person-to-person talk almost never is the listener recipient only. Almost never does the speaker say all he has to say in words. When your sister said of a newcomer, "Yes, he's good-looking, and he always has plenty to say for himself," how did you know, as surely as if she had proclaimed it, that she disliked the man? In this particular story on which you are working, how can you put on paper, either in the sentences themselves or in their accompanying tags, what will make a reader know that "he's good-looking" means "I detest him"?

"The word, a document wherein survives

"The record of a myriad myriad lives

"The word, the true foundation of the school,

"Logician's and philosopher's sole tool. . . .

"The ballad word which, sung by crowder blind,

"Thrill'd like a trumpet noble Sidney's mind;

"The homely word of Paston letters old,

"Wherein men pray, blaspheme, make love, and scold . .

"In that vernacular of English folk;

"The living word, redeeming still from death

"The spacious times of great Elizabeth;

"Miser of sound and syllable, no less than Midas of his coinage."

"The word leaps forth to life, a thing of soul,

"Working such wonders as, when rust and damp

"Were rubbed away, the Genius of the Lamp".

—Melville Best Anderson, The Happy Teacher

"The word, a document wherein survives
"The record of a myriad myriad lives
"The word, the true foundation of the school,
"Logician's and philosopher's sole tool. . . .
"The ballad word which, sung by crowder blind,
"Thrill'd like a trumpet noble Sidney's mind;
"The homely word of Paston Letters old,
"Wherein men pray, blaspheme, make love, and scold . . .
"The liquid word whose music Chaucer woke
"In that vernacular of English folk;
"The living word, redeeming still from death
" 'The spacious times of great Elizabeth':
"Wipe but the dust from parchment and from scroll,
"The word leaps forth to life, a thing of soul,
"Working such wonders as, when rust and damp
"Were rubbed away, the Genius of the Lamp."

       — Melville Best Anderson, *The Happy Teacher*

Words

I

"SCULPTURE is easy. All you do is take a piece of marble and knock off what you don't want."

In the same fashion, writing is easy. You dip your hand into the reservoir of words, bring up the ones you want and shake the unwanted ones off your fingers. In each instance, though, the difficulty is the same. What you do want is not to be determined until the knocking off and the shaking off are all but completed. Nearly every story in its early drafts distorts itself by unnecessary words — this quite apart from unnecessary detail or contradictory action. If five words in a sentence can be made to do the work of ten, then ten can do twice what they at first were doing. And one of the unchangeable facts a writer has always to face is that he can have only so many words in any story.

How many "so many" may be differs from story to story, but one condition remains true in all but the rarest cases. The "so many" is never as many as the writer uses in the beginning, never as many as in the beginning he feels he must use. Cutting merely for reduction of bulk is a form of revision rarely to be avoided. And this reduction is made not only, or even chiefly, with an eye on editorial limitations. It is made in order that the story may be intelligible enough, concise enough, to allow of any reader's following it to its conclusion.

The first forms of verbal revision to be considered, then, are those which emphasize the elimination of individual words. Most of such elimination, it is true, has to be done by feel, not by rule, but there exist both single words and phrases which, even when the writer himself finds no fault with them, are yet suspect by reason of their confirmed habit of being unnecessary.

Before he begins writing, a writer usually has some intuition about how long his whole story should be. His idea, he expects, should carry thus many or thus many words for its expression, will run thin, will shape up lumpily, if that number be much exceeded. In the early drafts, that number is exceeded, with the result that the story does exactly what was expected of it. By this time, however, its maker has become enamored of his phrases, so that no one of them seems to him superfluous, none clumsy, none wrongly placed.

A first help in finding which actually are wrongly

placed is time. A story as far finished as its writer
can finish it and then cooled by a week's or a month's
neglect shows sometimes, when it is brought to
light, whole paragraphs removable. A second help
is exploration, a few pages at a time, with attention
fixed at each reading upon one of the special weaknesses to which beginners are liable. One of these
weaknesses is the use of adjectives, and especially
the use of them in descriptive passages.

As the full circle of the moon passed behind its mourning veil of clouds, the garden was shrouded in shaggy
palms clustered in motionless groups, standing guard
in the pathless wilderness that pressed close around the
hacienda. Shiny-leaved banana trees no longer shim-
mered in the intermittent moonlight. The incessant
croaking of tree frogs ceased abruptly. Birds waited
softly in their nests. The garden was uneasily silent, as
if all nature were holding its breath. Beneath the op-
pressive stillness, the pounding of rebellious tides from
the coast vibrated in slow ominous undertones, a muf-
fled throbbing beneath the languorous mobility of the
tropics.

The morning sunshine broke gaily over the low mists
and showed the rocky cliffs emerging out of the white
foggy depths like grim Titans. Hardly distinguishable
from the natural eminences, the grey towers of a castle
loomed.

No one reading this book is likely to have been guilty of a passage as bad as either of the ones above. Lesser sins of the same nature, however, are all but invariable in unrevised manuscripts. Let us consider a few of the more usual ones as they appear in individual sentences.

A white swan floated in the still water.

In answer, a tall six-foot man got up from his chair.

Around him, tall trees seemed to brush the sky.

The light revealed wet, mossy walls with water trickling from top to bottom of them.

What the writer of each of these sentences is doing is, of course, translating a visual image into words. What he fails to do is to realize that one of the words he uses is implicit in another. "A white swan" — swans are white; when you think of a swan whiteness is part of your thought. A black swan is worth the adjective. So is a red-wing blackbird. So is a white crow. But when color, form, size, quality are the accustomed ones, they require no special mention. The awkward hippopotamus, the lumbering bear, the white lily — it is not because the adjectives are trite that they are ridiculous; they are ridiculous as well as trite because they are already tacitly expressed in the noun they accompany. And when an accompanying adjective says of the noun only what that noun can say unaided, a place has been discovered for word economy. Ordinarily, too, the economy brings about improvement other than that of saving space. "A swan floated on the still water"; "around him trees seemed to brush the sky" — either is more effective when disburdened of its modifier.

"Wet mossy walls, with water trickling . . ." is also repetitive, but this sentence contains still another superfluity, ". . . trickling from top to bottom of them." Try, in your imagination, to send water trickling from bottom to top. It is a feat not lightly accomplished. An early step in the verbal revision of any first draft is to go through it, page by page, and not too many pages at a sitting, looking for doubled statements, for statements false or obvious.

But that the meaning of one word is implicit in another does not always prove that either word should go. A phrase is not necessarily useless merely because it can be removed without impairment of meaning. Its usefulness may be for something quite other than meaning — for sound, for emphasis, for delay. Pater's dictum, "All art doth but consist in the removal of surplusage", is as safe a guide as on the day he wrote it, but the question of what is surplusage is no more answered now than it was then. Consider the two sentences below.

"The light revealed wet, mossy walls, with water trickling . . ."

"I pushed the button on my flash; a yellow, Chinese face was within a foot of my own."

Is "wet" in the first sentence superfluous? Almost certainly, yes. Is "yellow" in the second? Almost certainly, no. Chinese faces are yellow as regularly as swans are white, but the two words "yellow", "Chinese" give to the reader the two quick yet distinct shocks of recognition felt by the teller. Much more than meaning only must be considered in any revision. If Pater's sentence had read "Art consists in removing surplusage", it would have crowded its full sense into half the words, but it would also have slain its chances of survival.

After modifiers, connectives are the single words most in need of watching. *And* and *so* are chief offenders.

A distant flapping of wings, and she saw a flock of white birds flying low across the lake. Mary had never learned scientific names, and so she saw the birds simply as a moving mass which added a bright note to the dreary scene. She loved the brilliance of the birds, and she wanted —

He threw open the door, and a man was standing in the passage outside. Leaping back, he tried to shut the door again, and the man threw his whole weight against it.

In the first passage, any one *and* may be effective. Three of them in close succession cannot be. In the second, the clauses which *and* ties together are tied by force, not sense. When sense fails to aid the juncture, *and* is a connective always to be done away with, unless in dialogue or first-person telling where manner of speech is meant to mark the speaker. The repetitive use of *and* cannot, however, be brought under a general condemnation.

. . . and ran into the room and fell upon my knees before her and kissed her hands and dress and shoes and sobbed out my relief and pain and futile longing —

Every reader can recall passages where *and,* used and reused, sends the sentence hurrying along the page. These, however, are uses quite different from the monotonous tying together of one clause and one clause, such as marks the first of the passages quoted.

Unlike *and,* an overused *so,* that first recourse of

feeble minds, has no advantages unless, as with *and,* it be in dialogue or first-person telling.

She was afraid he would come and talk to her, so she went into the house.

They pulled the rope tight so it would not slip.

Burt knew the road, so they got safely to the first stopping place.

Reasons could be adduced against the use of *so* in any of the three sentences given, but the major reason lies in the failure to assert importances over unimportances in the sentence, and in the feebleness of sound to which each *so* adds its share.

Modifiers and connectives having been looked to, subordinate clauses come next under scrutiny, especially those beginning with *which*.

The color of the house was a dull grey, which gave it a sullen, dark appearance which was distasteful to her.

The signpost which he had seen first had pointed in a different direction from the second, which confused him a good deal.

A sound which was scarcely distinct enough to be heard roused him from the reverie which had been absorbing him.

Stumbling up the stairs to his room, which was on the second floor, he realized . . .

The first, second, and third of the sentences given above contain each two *which's;* each *which* in each sentence possesses a separate antecedent. If such an arrangement makes for effectiveness, there is, of course no reason why it should not be used, but a sentence so provided has ordinarily a pair of drawbacks. It sets a *which* and a *which* (as ugly a word as language holds) neighboring on each other; and it raises to the importance of a clause what a modifier or a phrase often could express even better.

The color of the house, a dull grey, gave it a sullen, dark appearance distasteful to her.

There are other forms for the statement, according to whether the writer's purpose is to emphasize the dreary look or the effect of that look upon the person. No one of the forms, though, demands a duplication of *which's.*

—which confused him a good deal.

Here the *which* has its antecedent only in the general idea of the clause preceding, not in a particular word. Again, the pronouncement against such a usage is a pronouncement only, not a ukase. There

exist sentences demanding a loose *which* and profit-
ing by it. But in his own work a writer is called
on to look twice at *which's* thus dangling. Now
and then his sentence demands it; oftener what
demands it is his own unwillingness to labor on the
reshaping of the sentence into a form less awkward,
more economical.

A sound which was scarcely distinct enough to be
heard roused him from the reverie which had been
absorbing him.

Should both the *which's* be removed? Or is one
needed for placing of emphasis? What arrangement
of words will place a chief importance on "sound"?
What will give "reverie" importance?

The fourth example, however, is the one deserving
of the longest pause on the part of any reader. Observe it in four forms.

Stumbling up the stairs to his room, which was on the
second floor . . .

Stumbling up the stairs to his room on the second
floor . . .

Stumbling up the stairs to his second-floor room . . .

Stumbling up to his second-floor room . . .

More often than not, sentences made by an inexpert hand are overloaded with clauses as well as with modifiers. To reduce clause to phrase, phrase to single word, saves space and concentrates meaning. There are sentences where, for the sake of sound or emphasis, the clause, though readily reducible, should still remain a clause, but these are the exceptions. No inexperienced writer can afford to take it for granted that the heavy and rotund sentences of his first draft are among them.

Three fourths of verbal revision is elimination. The other fourth goes to the strengthening of the words remaining. With modifiers reduced in number, nouns and verbs carry a greater weight, require therefore a more careful selection. Use of the weakling verb propped on each side by modifiers is especially a beginner's habit. Observe the fashion in which modifier has been absorbed by verb in the sentences following — not, it may be pointed out, sentences by beginners.

Freen fidgeted around the room. He pawed over the books on the table, the sheet music on the piano. Finally his anxiety blustered out into words.

"And then that boy, that young . . ." The sudden drop of his voice elided the epithet. 'That boy' was prancing down the veranda towards them.

A sound squeezed its way through the silence. She sat up, breathing hard, her frightened eyes searching the room.

None of these sentences contain extraordinary or fanciful uses of words. Any reader can select sentences like them from almost any page he reads. Considering the examples — the ones here given or his own — he cannot fail to recognize the compactness, the sense of movement, given to a sentence by verbs which suggest at once the action and its quality or cause. Not many writers are better at this suggestiveness than Henry James. Observe the verbs and their modifiers in the following passage from "The Real Thing." *

"I've come from Mr. Rivet," the lady said at last . . .
"Ah, Claude Rivet recommended me?" I inquired; and I added that it was very kind of him, though I could reflect that, as he only painted landscape, this was not a sacrifice.
The lady looked very hard at the gentleman, and the gentleman looked around the room. Then, staring at the floor a moment and stroking his mustache, he rested his pleasant eyes on me with the remark: "He said you were the right one."
"I try to be, when people want to sit."

* From *The Real Thing and Other Stories,* by Henry James. By permission of The Macmillan Company, publishers

"Yes, we should like to," said the lady anxiously.

"Do you mean together?"

My visitors exchanged a glance. "If you could do anything with *me,* I suppose it would be double," the gentleman stammered.

"Oh, yes, there's naturally a higher charge for two figures than for one."

"We should like to make it pay," the husband confessed.

"That's very good of you," I returned, appreciating so unwonted a sympathy — for I supposed he meant pay the artist.

A sense of strangeness seemed to dawn on the lady. "We mean for the illustrations — Mr. Rivet said you might put one in."

"Put one in — an illustration?" I was equally confused.

"Sketch her off, you know," said the gentleman, coloring . . .

"Ah, you're — you're — a — ?" I began, as soon as I had mastered my surprise. I couldn't bring out the dingy word "models"; it seemed to fit the case so little.

"We haven't had much practice," said the lady.

"We've got to *do* something, and we've thought that an artist in your line might perhaps make something of us," her husband threw off. He further mentioned that they didn't know many artists and that they had gone first, on the off-chance (he painted views, of course, but sometimes put in figures — perhaps I remembered) to

Mr. Rivet, whom they had met a few years before at a place in Norfolk where he was sketching.

"We used to sketch a little ourselves," the lady hinted.

"It's very awkward, but we absolutely *must* do something," her husband went on.

"Of course, we're not so *very* young," she admitted, with a wan smile.

At the other end of the scale from Henry James is, of course, Hemingway. Practicing an economy as effective though entirely different in kind, his repeated *said's* send his sentences shooting like bullets from the page. In "The Killers" *, two strangers have taken possession of a lunch room, waiting for their prospective victim to come in for supper and talking meanwhile with the counter-boy, over whom one of them is keeping guard.

"All right," George said. "What are you going to do with us afterward?"

"That'll depend," Max said. "That's one of those things you never know at the time."

George looked up at the clock. It was a quarter past six. The door from the street opened. A streetcar motorman came in.

"Hello, George," he said. "Can I get supper?"

"Sam's gone out," George said. "He'll be back in about half an hour."

* From *Men Without Women,* by Ernest Hemingway. By permission of Charles Scribner's Sons, publishers

"I'd better go up the street," the motorman said. George looked at the clock. It was twenty minutes past six.

"That was nice, bright boy," Max said. "You're a regular little gentleman."

"He knew I'd blow his head off," Al said from the kitchen.

"No," said Max. "It ain't that. Bright boy is nice. He's a nice boy. I like him."

At six-fifty-five George said: "He's not coming."

The suave irony of the first passage, the bantering and callous ferocity of the second — neither, naturally, lies entirely in the verbs. The arrangement of the words, the adjectives or the conspicuous lack of adjectives — these and other sentence elements must also be taken into consideration. But to a considerable degree, the verbs themselves are responsible for the tone achieved. A non-writer's favorite reply here is, "But you cannot contrast the two pieces of writing. The writers were trying to do different things." They were; but, whatever they were trying to do, words were their medium. Anyone familiar with stories badly written will recall scenes of desperate action, scenes of supposed suavity, which, alike, lay flat on the page, lines of written syllables and no more. Along with emotional and intellectual responses to story material must go always the patient placing and replacing of words to make them express those responses.

But though the weakness of certain word uses are evident enough when they are pointed out in a given sentence, how are you to be sure of them when they are not pointed out? How are you to find them in your own work? If you really are newly come to writing, probably it is best to put your earliest efforts on other people's sentences. What of the *and's* and *so's*, the *which's, very's,* and *quite's,* and other adverbs and adjectives in the sentences below — sentences, all of them, clipped from the stories of amateurs? How far, merely by disburdening a sentence, can you improve it? How far can you improve it by altering the order of its remaining words?

It was late one August night when she knocked at our door.

A deep breath now and then and the occasional shifting of some weary body on the hard rough flooring was all that disturbed the uncommunicative mood that seemed to have fallen on the few derelict humans seeking shelter there.

Sprawling roots curled around his feet like coiled creatures as he stumbled through the rough-barked trees, interlaced with unresisting vines.

We had spent seven consecutive summers at Laguna, which made it hard now for us to give up going again.

Mother had just about given up the whole idea of finding a house, and was beginning to think of ways in which she could reconcile us to staying in town for the next three months, when Joan and I decided to do some very vigorous house-hunting on our own, for we were quite determined to find a place.

The river rolled very smoothly onward and swirled in innumerable patterns around twigs and rocks which it carried along in its easy, effortless current toward the security of the open sea.

Several minutes passed, while various members of her party tried to persuade her, and finally she allowed herself to be led off through the doorway leading into the lobby. The curtain dropped to show a passage of fifteen minutes, and, as it rose again, the scene was the same as before.

Remember, as you read these examples, that there is no such thing as one inevitably right form for any sentence. There are only forms more or less clear, more or less forceful, more or less pleasant to eye and ear. Remember too that when a particular word in a sentence is wrong, it is not because of grammarians' pronouncements against it but because it confuses sense or wastes space or produces unpleasantness in sound. If it does not do these things, it ceases to be wrong, for grammar and syntax are not dictators over words but only recorders of their reputable uses. Both, however, are recorders worth watching. "Mere grammar is twisted into the nature of the language about as mere gravitation is twisted into that of the physical universe," and an eye on mere grammar will prevent both unconscious awkwardnesses and those which the perpetrator has fondly thought of as "style." Not many people need consciously concern themselves with "style" at any time. None need till after they have attained a decent mastery over the tools of their trade.

II

"In an inexplicable suicide, for which there is no known motive . . ."

San Francisco Chronicle

Disburdening a set of sentences is sometimes all that is needed for turning bad writing into good. This disburdening, however, is not necessarily limited to the removal of words, discussed in the preceding section, or to the cutting off of clauses repetitious to absurdity, as in the sentence given above. Quite as often, it can be accomplished only by a clarification of the writer's thought in regard either to the material of his story or to his reader's approach to the story.

Several times that night Johnson expected the old man to die, but he clung doggedly to life with a strange persistence.

She suffered intensely in her child's suffering, because she loved him with the devotion which mothers give to their children.

Sitting out dances made her unhappy, for she did not like to be neglected.

Any one of the three statements is an assault on the reader's intelligence, for in each the maker of the sentence has turned the general into the particular, presenting a universal condition as though it were a special case.

An assault on the reader's intelligence too is the overloading not only of a sentence with words but of a passage with details.

The rancid odor of grease nauseated him as he opened the heavy door; he heard the familiar whining cry of a hungry child. With a feeble gesture of disgust . . .

He recognized the old rowboat floundering, water-logged, on a greyish patch of filthy sand, the small dirty wharf sagging in the slime. The putrid odor of stagnant water assailed him.

The writer is trying too hard. In prose as in painting, it is impossible to put every leaf on the tree. A few of them may safely be left for the reader's imagination to supply. The diction appropriate to a particular story depends upon the kind of story, upon the kind of reader, but the "lean, terse style" is one towards which most beginners can profitably struggle. Even when, after a revision or two, some of the repetitions and ornamentations are put back into paragraphs earlier denuded of them, the practice of deciding upon their removal, upon their retention, is practice of the best.

It was quite by accident that Ada North happened to buy that particular book. It wasn't the sort of thing she was in the habit of reading. She never was sure what obscure impulse within her prompted her to do such a thing. But she *did* buy the book, and it was responsible for the whole thing.

It all started upon a very stormy Saturday afternoon soon after lunch. She had gone back to the office to finish up some important details for Mr. Grigsby. She really could have let those papers go until Monday, but Ada was an exceptionally efficient secretary who believed implicitly in the motto, "Never put off until tomorrow what you can do today." She often told the younger girls in the office that that was one of the important maxims of a good secretary. If she had not returned to the office, she would not have received Homer's message until she had gone home; and so, of course, she would never have bought that book.

As Claire dressed, she pictured in her mind the entrance she would make when Philip came. It was seven-thirty, and he would arrive for eight o'clock dinner. She could make a very nice entrance if she could go down the stairway — sort of glide down — with him at the bottom, looking up, waiting for her. That would be rather graceful. But then again, it would probably be more convenient if she just let Etta take him into the library when he came. She might not be ready by the time he arrived. And then he could talk to Father until she came downstairs.

All of the increasing group centered around the drowned boy, who was laid on blankets on the sand. The other fishermen started working on him, while the woman had to be wrenched from her son by the two men who had accompanied her. Insufferable minutes ensued. He seemed most certainly dead, responding to no treatment. But no, his eyelids moved. No, it was just an accident. Yes, he was alive.

Everyone was excited. People pressed closer. Yes, he seemed all right now. He was breathing regularly and already a little warmth returned to his body. All he needed now was plenty of rest and he ought to pull through. Some one seemed to be taking the initiative. Matters were taking on a more commonplace air, so that gradually the crowd began to drop away.

In each of the three passages above, count the number of restatements not of word but of idea. In the opening paragraph of the first one, Ada North happens to buy a book, does not usually buy that kind of book, is not sure why she buys it, but — climax of the paragraph — does buy it. The second paragraph is as bad, stating and restating the fact of Ada's meticulousness. These restatements are not the repetitions meant to drive home to a reader's mind the various importances of a story. They are no more than the unwinding into words of a heavy and unilluminated mind. In the first and third passages especially, note the mind's attempt to escape from labor by retreat into loose and general terms — ". . . the whole thing. It all started. . . . Some one seemed to be taking the initiative. Matters were taking on a commonplace air." Even without the fold on fold of restatement, this is wording murderous to reader's interest.

Oliver Kendrick stood listlessly by the windows. He eyed the dull sandstone building across the street, looking uninterestedly at the white-coated dentist dimly visible behind a smudged gilt sign. Far up, a drab brown figure hung precariously by slender straps, one hand clutching a heavy bucket and the other busily scouring a dirty window pane. Below him, the frowsy head of a stenographer rose and fell, rose and fell, in little, uneasy

jerks as she bent and straightened over her machine. A
film of dirty cloud bridged the space between the buildings.

The paragraph above is the opening for a story
of disillusionment and ruin. Again, the writer of
it is trying too hard, but this time his mode of trying
calls for a more detailed analysis. In the story, Oliver is considering suicide and suicide by the incon-
siderate method of hurtling from his window down
to the street below. He is entitled, therefore, to
turn upon the scene in front of him a jaundiced
eye. Dreary and repulsive that street would un-
doubtedly look to Oliver. His maker's theory, then,
is this: Whatever meets Oliver's gaze will take the
color of the eye regarding it. Let him look out on
the street. Set down one thing he sees, another, still
another. When you have set down enough, each
tinged by Oliver's somber view, the cumulative
effect will produce in a reader some part of Oliver's
emotion. It will — unless, long before that emotion
is produced, the reader has revolted and produced
an emotion of his own towards the whole story.

The "look-by-look" method of writing which
Oliver illustrates does occasionally do exactly what
it is intended to do, but it is a method easy to over-
use and especially in the opening paragraph of a

story. Intense emotion of any kind, unless it be the emotion of curiosity, lies always close to absurdity. Insistence on emotion at the beginning of a story, multiplying and remultiplying of details meant to produce it, is work for a practiced hand. Between being appalled at Oliver's plight and being amused at the author's attempt to appall you, the distance is perilously short.

The overburdening of the passages shown thus far has come, in general, from the writer's fear that he will not hold readers' attention long enough at a stretch to produce the effect he wants. A struggle for effect harder to define, much harder to alter, is that which shows itself in precious writing.

At what point writing becomes precious, how much ornament a given style, a given subject, can carry, is a thing individually to be decided, and less from story to story than from writer to writer. A powerful mind, a sweep of feeling, a wide experience deeply pondered — these things make possible to their possessor use of images and special adaptations of words which a meaner endowment may not risk. But for most stories and most writers, deliberate ornamentation needs much scrutiny before it is allowed a place in finished work. Phrases pushing up like mushrooms above the level of the narrative have

a habit of turning out to be toadstools on later in-
spection. "Take out whatever you particularly like"
is hard counsel, but oftener than not it is wise
counsel as well.

To me, the new store appeared as a plate-glass, cello-
phane-wrapped, linoleumned palace.

The life in her was guarded from anguish by a china
fine body, and she always wore pale chiffon in the evening, palest pink and blue and lavender. Tonight she was
wearing lavender and her vital fire was burning high.

He came from nowhere and from everywhere—a
wandering man with his violin. About him the lure of
far places; in his strange, dark eyes too much knowledge,
perhaps of love. And it was spring when he came to the
village.

A ladder of moonbeams reached to the couch, the
light of its beauty revealing the incongruity of one slip-
pered and one nude foot.

Preciousness in each of these passages drops to
prettifying, to a wearying struggle for originality
disadvantageous to both reader and writer. On the
reader's side, the wording distracts him from what
the writer is trying to say; a story is not made up of
a phrase plus a phrase any more than it is made up
of an incident plus an incident. On the writer's side,
excessive care for the pictorial quality of words,

continual conscious struggle for the striking phrase, results often in loss of spontaneity. A piddling habit grows from story to story till at last idea is habitually subordinated to expression. For the excerpts shown here, cutting and the substitution of phrases less tortured and elaborated will redeem them. For their writers, there is redemption only through a patient study of the values of simplicity. With every beginner at writing, the attempt to make sentences say exactly what he means comes far in advance of the attempt to make them say it with elaboration.

Simplicity is not identical with commonplaceness. Preciousness pushes language above the level of the emotion or the information it has to carry. Wording actually commonplace is that which falls below the emotional level of its substance, that which is vague, inaccurate, shopworn.

"Isn't it quiet?" The whispered question gave the guide quite a start.

The guide is planning to murder the whisperer. That "quite a start" makes farcical both his feeling and the laboriously manufactured situation.

She was sort of afraid he would come after her, and she did not know what she would do if he did.

It seemed to her he must be badly hurt, so she began to cry and scream.

Unlike preciousness, the elimination of common-placeness in diction is not to be accomplished by the reworking of particular passages. What does accomplish it, and that only most gradually, is the development through reading and listening of a sensitiveness to the effect of words.

He felt he had to leave, though doings at the party were just well under way.

Here is commonplaceness again but commonplace-ness of a different kind. Only a reader of abnormally lively imagination can translate "doings at the party" into visual image. The writer's failure to make the translation himself was probably the reason for his phrasing. No rule is safe to follow always, but the rule that presentations in a story should be specific comes as near to being always a safe guide as any rule can.

"Dr. Anderson was well dressed" gives the reader next to nothing; "Dr. Anderson buttoned his expensive tweed coat . . ." There is material for making a picture. "The way she was dressed made her look cool even in all the heat." "She was in white from neck to shoes." "He made as much noise inside the room as he could, trying to attract the other man's attention." "He shouted, 'Bill! Bill!' at the top of his lungs, and beat his fists against the door."

Failure to particularize is most often the result of mental laziness. Mental laziness accounts, too, for the borrowing habit conspicuous among dealers in the commonplace. "Came the dawn" has at last been laughed out of existence, but successors to it appear, each a burr stuck to the manuscript of some writer who longs for originality but knows himself unable to produce it. Any writer may be sure that a striking phrase, a striking word arrangement, fathered by someone else has not met his eyes alone. It will reappear in his story and in enough others to make it presently anathema to readers.

The habit of borrowing other people's phrases is a dishonesty easily recognized and easily discontinued. Less easy to discontinue is the habit of letting your own chosen words tell something other than the truth. "Horizons Are Always Green", the title of a recent amateur story, is an example of infringement on truth flagrant enough for instant recognition. The writer's love of a phrase, his muddled recollection of some axiom about far fields, left his common sense in abeyance.

She stretched her hands to the fire, nearly burning her fingers in cupping a small chin.

To the writer of a sentence such as this, "Try it" is as good advice as can be given. An attempt to act out the scene others are expected to accept would presumably have left his heroine less of a contortionist. Common sense should suggest to any writer that, either in imagination or by bodily act, he find out whether he is telling the truth about his character's postures and actions.

Accuracy in daily observation is still another necessity if words are to be truthfully used. "Willows whiten, aspens quiver," wrote Tennyson a couple of generations ago, and made visible for the first time to a million readers the changing color of a willow's leaves when the wind turns them. ". . . the live oaks quivering and shuddering outside her windows" wrote a less scrupulous observer in description of the most stable, the most unquivering of trees. Observation is cultivatable; where cultivation has not yet gone far it is worth while to verify statements before they reach their final place on the page.

Whenever the conversation turned to the beauties of the world, Mary would say to her friends, "I never could see anything so marvelous about nature. I've sat and positively stared . . ."

Mary's maker is not intentionally assigning to her a role more repetitive than that of the Three Bears. He has done no more than fail to understand the effect upon a sentence of *whenever* and *would,* and so has said what he had no purpose of saying.

Muddled thinking, as exemplified in "Horizons Are Always Green", guesswork presentation of material supposedly factual, stating of the specific as though it were the general — these three things account for perhaps half the verbal untruths which find their way into stories.

The other half is accounted for by the slipshod and ungrammatical use of individual words. The writer who speaks of quivering live oaks may defend his choice of adjective or may plead imperfect noticing. The writer who permits the teller of his story to say, "There was something in his manner which seemed to inflame me," has no shield for his incompetence. Neither has the writer who announces his hero as "dull and disinterested because of the heat." A dictionary is the one book indispensable on any beginner's shelf. A handbook on English composition may well sit beside it. Neither is an infallible guide, but both assist in keeping sharp the edges of meaning, the finer points of usage. And for a writer, to use words truthfully is quite as important as to tell the truth with the ones he uses.

There is, however, one propensity of English words against which a beginner, striving to use his word truthfully, has forever to be on guard. This is their habit of picking up additional meanings. The denotation and the connotation of a word may be far apart. Of connotations, there may be many, and many times a given connotation may be stronger than the word's original meaning. Ford Madox Ford, in *Joseph Conrad, A Personal Remembrance,* speaks of Conrad's impassioned prejudice against this slipperiness.

Conrad's indictment of the English language was this, that no English word is a word; that all English words are instruments for exciting blurred emotions. "Oaken" in French means "made of oak wood" — nothing more. "Oaken" in English connotes innumerable moral attributes: it will connote stolidity, resolution, honesty, blond features, relative unbreakableness, absolute unbendableness — also, made of oak. . . . The consequence is that no English word has clean edges.*

To cleanse the edges, the utmost a writer can do is to keep his eyes and ears awake to contemporary

* From *Joseph Conrad: A Personal Remembrance,* by Ford Madox Ford. By permission of Albert and Charles Boni, Inc., publishers

usage and to make the surroundings of his doubtful word such that the intended connotation is inevitable. "She flew to meet her lover." Did she
hurry or did she take passage on an airplane?

III

Seeing her standing smiling there, he stopped, smiling himself at her gracious unspoken greeting.

The hissing and grinding sentence above was
constructed by a usually careful writer and was
published in a reputable magazine. It is reproduced
here as exemplification of a truth every writer comes
early to know. Reading over his manuscript, he will
pass by sentences which later, seen in print, are
sufficient to set the teeth on edge. Stevenson speaks
of finding himself "riding the flat *a*" through the
length of a page. Sometimes it is the flat *a;* sometimes, as in the sentence above, it is *s* and *g*. Sometimes it is not a sound but a phrase. There are passages in Chesterton's essays in which the qualifying
A certain — "A certain pleasure . . . a certain doubt
. . . a certain reservation . . . a certain author" —
begins to affect the reader as the modifier "good ole",
tacked to every noun, affected Penrod Scofield's
companions.

Sometimes, instead of a single phrase, it is a flock of one-syllable words, or a flock of two-syllable ones, word accents and sense accents falling at different points. Sometimes it is a series of sentences made all to the same monotonous measure. In third-person telling always, and usually in first-person telling as well, repeated use destroys the effectiveness of any sentence form. If a writer's ear does not make that announcement to him, then he must either give up fiction or slowly cultivate the capacity for hearing sentence rhythms.

Ugliness in writing is limited to no one kind. And just as there is no one ugliness, there is no one cure. The nearest to a general panacea is the beginner's persistent reading aloud of his work, reading it softly, without listeners and without oratory; reading it, if he can, as intently, as dispassionately, as a doctor fingers down the vertebræ of the spine in search of injury.

But reading his own work aloud can improve it only up to the level of the reader's taste. For raising that level, there is no substitute for the reading of other people's prose and good prose at that.

What "good" consists of is capable of no final definition; a working definition, however, is easy to reach. For a given writer at any given moment, good prose is that which he recognizes as better than his own, that which awakens admiration and desire for emulation, and which he reads and re-reads for the love of reading it. What it will be nobody can tell. Nobody can tell, either, how many times his taste may change, transforming what once was stirring into bombast, what once was touching into bathos. It is a safe guess, though, that he will be correct in believing the prose which delights him at the moment to be prose better than the prose he writes. If he can find it, if he can read it in soli-tude, trying over a sentence aloud, picking out a phrase, vocalizing it, repeating it, ringing it in the air, he is doing as much as can be done for his own improvement. If he can do it not for the sake of improvement but out of sheer love, his case is better still, for not many people are capable of writing who are incapable of a single-minded delight in the sound of words.

Analysis of effective phrases is not in question here. What is in question is only the rejoicing recog-nition of their qualities. Nobody ever learned to write whose recognitions were not more often in-stinctive than reasoned. Analysis of ugly phrases, on the other hand, does have a limited value. In the passages considered in the earlier sections of this chapter, it was evident that not all of the ugliness of ugly sentences came from the words alone. Much of it came from the relationships between words. Change the order of words in some familiar line, and this truth is instantly exemplified.

"Time like a many-colored dome of glass . . ."

"Time like a dome of many-colored glass . . ."

Nobody with an ounce of writing feeling can doubt which line the poet wrote. And in prose, the placing of words is no less important than in verse. Certain principles concerning this placing are taught most children in grade school. Many adults, however, need to relearn them.

One of these principles is that you cannot alter the normal word order of English sentences without paying for your alterations. What that normal order is? Let us look at a few decent but undistinguished sentences and see.

The dark, cloudy sky promised rain.

A handsome, sullen boy stood beside me, waiting for the storm to cease.

Mary walked into the classroom and sat down in a last row seat in order to have a good view of the other students as they arrived.

In all three, we have the accustomed form of English speech and of English writing — the one from which the exceptions, though frequent, remain exceptions still.

The sky, dark, cloudy, promised rain.

Beside me, waiting for the storm to cease, stood a boy, handsome, sullen.

It is apparent to any reader that the sky has become more threatening, the boy's sullenness been increased by the change in word order. As for Mary and her last row seat — but Mary is left for the reader's rearrangement. What is evident from the first two sentences is this: Give to a word an unusual place in a sentence and you give it thereby an added emphasis, an added importance.

And I remembered how, long ago, I had paused and wondered on that same bridge.

Return the "long ago" to the end of the sentence. You have shortened the elapsed time by years.

When, therefore, a writer pushes a word out of its place, he does so, if he is wise, because that word is of special note, not because he is erratically trying for originality. If the word is not of an importance equal to its special placing, what he accomplishes is the confusion of his readers and, still more disastrous, the further confusion of his own feeling for word values.

There are other grammar-school precepts useful to remember: that words connected in thought should, as often as possible, be kept together in a sentence; that the beginning and end of the sentence, the beginning and end of the paragraph, offer placings of unusual prominence. Ugly passages, tested against these simplicities, often lose their conspicuous ugliness. For any advance beyond the loss of ugliness, word placing must be done by ear. That "unremitting, never discouraged care for the shape and ring of sentences" advised by Joseph Conrad is every writer's necessity. Trying the sentences over in the story you are now at work on, is their tune right? Trying them in little groups, seldom more than a page at a time, do they have the ring you want? If they do not, is it because of wordiness, of preciousness, of commonplaceness, of word arrangement?

Of the sentences below, so far as a sentence can be judged apart from its context, which were written by skilled and which by unskilled hands? And what in the sentence influences your judgment?

Brick by brick he had built it himself, working evenings and Sundays.

For a solid hour he had been contemplating imminent death.

Her long face was innocent, indeed ignorant, of cosmetics.

In fact, once thought of, the thought needed little verification, for, as Clarice realized, it was exactly what any person with a trace of exhibitionism in his make-up — and all of us have the trace — would do.

It must have taken me, for my broken, difficult account, half an hour.

After a while I said, "I'm sorry that I won't be here to see her, but we're leaving tomorrow and probably we won't be back until Christmas."

Tufts of golden hair peeked out from below her trim little hat.

"Listen — " Both men stiffened automatically; the sailor at the wheel, tightening his grasp on the spokes nervously, watched the officers anxiously.

It was not as deep as it had looked nor as he had feared it was.

Conclusion: To Place a Story

THERE are three ways of placing stories. One is to sell them. One is to dispose of them to some Little Magazine which offers publication and sometimes prestige but no pay. One is to stow them in trunks or bottom bureau drawers, leaving them there against the time of the writer's further ripening. This very brief chapter purposes to consider these three ways in inverse order.

A good deal is to be said in behalf of the trunk and the bureau drawer. Especially, a good deal is to be said for them in the instances of those persons who have the patience and the ability ultimately to become writers. Somerset Maugham speaks, in *The Summing Up*, of having been kept by some blessed misfortune from exploiting a subject before he knew enough to handle it. Many writers less eminent have had the same experience. In *To Use a Book*, it is explained and underlined that early writing efforts are usually exercises, not stories.

●

The suitable refuge for an exercise is a storage place from which it may be drawn from time to time for encouraging contrast with its maker's later work.

The Little Magazines, coming into existence and going out of it again with a bewildering rapidity, may provide important helps for a beginner or, as readily, they may be his chief hindrances. The help comes from their offering him a chance to see how his story looks in print, frequently a chance for critical comment from their editors, and now and then the high encouragement of having his work noticed in places other than that of its first appearance. The hindrances spring from the fact that often the staffs and supporters of Little Magazines are grievance groups, people devoted to a single *ism,* people convinced that congeries of writers other than their own are necessarily worshipers of Rimmon. These are attitudes of mind singularly contagious. Grievance, self-conceit, inability to distinguish good from bad unless each wear a given label are disabilities which under any set of circumstances are always in act of creeping up on a writer. During his apprentice years especially, the writing company he keeps should be company broad-minded, tolerant, with no purpose of regi-

menting newcomers. If he is debarred from keeping this company, it is better for him to have no
writing company at all.

The Little Magazines devoted to regional interests are more likely than their fellows to escape
this curse of over-righteousness, since they possess
a reason for existence other than scorn of their
contemporaries. Some of the rest escape too, but
so swiftly do they appear and disappear that which
these "some" are a beginner has to decide for himself. His decision is important, for any periodical
welcoming his work is certain to exercise on him
a strong influence, one finally advantageous or finally stultifying. And in all his first years of practice, growth is many times more important to
him than is publication.

Attempting to publish, however, even from the
first awkward endeavor, has no unavoidable harm
in it, unless it be to the editorial staffs involved.
To the beginner, the continual sending out of
manuscripts is harmful only insofar as it consumes
his time and distracts his attention, or as it piles
up in him a sense of injury.

This last is a danger not to be minimized. There
is no town, there is scarcely a village, which does
not number among its inhabitants some would-

be writer indignantly certain that worth in fiction is being overlooked in favor of distinguished names, and ready, with small encouragement, to point out, in any issue of any magazine, stories far inferior to the ones he impatiently mails and remails. In some very small measure, too, he is justified. A distinguished name does predispose an editor to acceptance. It does because it also predisposes readers to reading. A reader prefers to know something of the writer to whom he surrenders his time exactly as a patient prefers to know something of the surgeon to whom he surrenders his appendix. Any other attitude would be unreasonable — as unreasonable as the not infrequent attitude of the disappointed struggler with fiction who feels that because he wants to write, therefore some audience ought to want to read his writing.

The point is worth emphasis because attitude of mind is what writing springs from. The sullen, the self-pitying, the grudge-bearing attitude is that much more weight to carry against competitors less burdened. Ordinarily, too, the weight is carried unnecessarily. No beginner who has acquired even a passable degree of competence is in danger of being long overlooked. Stories of substance, stories well planned, well written, which yet fail of publication probably do exist. They are rarer, though, than white blackbirds. When a would-be writer has energetically pursued his craft through a three- or four-year apprenticeship and has at last produced a really good story, he can supply himself with stamps and envelopes in a mood of entire tranquillity. His really good story may not stay with the first editor to whom he sends it, nor yet with the second, but it will stay somewhere.

For his own peace of mind and the saving of his time, he will do well to make out, before his first sending, a list of all available magazines, beginning with those he does not actually hope to attain and ending with the ones he is accustomed to despise. Then, the manuscript returning from one editor, he slides it immediately into a fresh envelope and starts it towards another. Whether he sends it out himself or finds an agent to send it for him, whether its corners are dog-eared or immaculate, its success will be about the same. If there is power or mirth or pathos in it, it will not reach the end of the list. The way to place a story is to write one.

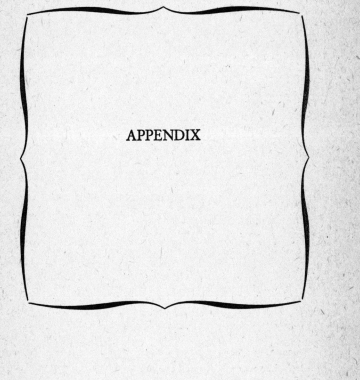

APPENDIX

Appendix

I

Minnie

MINNIE was born and brought up in Raeder. If you think you know a worse fate, produce it for comparison.

Her mother, whose relation to the Caesar ladies was tolerably distant, dispensed with her husband about the time that Minnie was learning to creep. Later, she married another husband and dispensed with him, and later still eschewed matrimony and took to restaurant keeping.

Minnie took her infant naps in a clothesbasket under the long restaurant counter. She shed her infant teeth in vain attempts on "steak-'r-chops", dressed up T-bones for dolls, and fought with cats outside the back entrance for the safety of her creations.

About the time she was able to outwit the cats, she became old enough simultaneously for school and dishwashing. After that, she was a factor in economic conditions. Raeder has something less than a thousand inhabitants, each of whom knows or knows about all the rest. No teacher was ever so unreasonable as to expect excellence of "that Gans girl", and no teacher ever got from her more than she expected. Dishwashing, on the other hand, might fairly be called a gift by inheritance. She prospered exceedingly at it. She added a rough and ready knowledge of cookery almost by instinct, and that capacity for scrubbing without the removal of dirt which is a near approach to genius. By the time she was sixteen, she could carry five full meals deftly balanced between wrist and shoulder, she could serve up short orders with the maximum of speed, and she had developed an admiration for her mother which was almost a passion.

————————

1. The four paragraphs above cover sixteen years of time. What are the phrases by means of which the writer keeps the reader aware of time's passage?

2. What excerpt quoted in *Time* uses a similar method?

3. ". . . with every story, he, the writer, faces the question of how to crowd into his first paragraphs an extra ten years or so of his person's experience." What are some of the devices by which the author of "Minnie" fits in needed information?

4. Rewrite the passage, using minute-to-minute treat-

ment but keeping the rewritten account within the space now allowed it. What means can you find for so keeping it?

5. What is the point of observation from which "Minnie" is written? Note the sentences which prove your assertion to be right.

6. In *Points of Observation,* p. 88, are listed the ways in which the story of X, Y, and Mrs. Y may be told. So far as the paragraphs given show, which of these ways are precluded by the material of this story?

7. "Her mother, who was a woman of doubtful character, was separated from her husband when Minnie was eight months old." Contrast this sentence with the original. The two are identical in sense. What does the original sentence do which this one does not?

8. What is the value of the word "tolerably" where it now stands?

9. Pick three words other than "tolerably" which make large contribution to the tone of the excerpt as well as to its meaning.

10. What tone does the excerpt have?

11. Rewrite one paragraph, giving it another tone consistently sustained.

Mr. Simms

Mr. Simms reached over the side of his bed and turned off the alarm clock with a grunt of displeasure. He did not feel rested. He wanted to sleep a few more hours yet; he knew he'd have a bad day if he arose feeling tired. But he must face facts; a business man can afford himself no dilly-dallying about in bed in the morning. It was seven o'clock. He must get up. He arose and walked over to the window which looked out upon a gray and cheerless morning fog. Another drizzly day, he remarked to himself. A pity that the sun never shone in San Francisco.

He arrived at the breakfast table four minutes earlier than usual. Mr. Simms always kept track of the time, all day long. It made one's day more organized, somehow. He liked to keep track of the minutes as he dressed in the morning, as he ate his breakfast, his lunch, and his dinner. There was no time for minute-wasting in the world of business!

Adjusting the pince-nez on the high bony ridge of his nose, Mr. Simms snorted mildly at the scrambled eggs before him. Too moist; hadn't he told her a hundred times in the last five years that he couldn't eat them when they were too moist! And the toast! But Mr. Simms did not like to complain of things when Sarah looked cross. For then she would fly into a rage, refuse to finish whatever she was doing, and declare wrathfully that she would leave and find some place else to work. He remembered this particular speech of hers. It was the same every time, but she had never left. She had, in fact, threatened to leave only three or four times during the past five years. It would be unpleasant if she did ever get it into her head to go. It would be unpleasant getting used to having someone new around. There was something rather comfortable and familiar about having the same person there every day. Sarah's extravagantly plump figure and her old, rather tired face was a part of Mr. Simms' order of things. Without her, his routine would be entirely disrupted.

———————

1. The paragraphs quoted form the opening of a story dealing with one day in Mr. Simms' life. As it is now written, the passage contains 370 words. Bring it down to 200 without loss of substance or change in the presentation of Mr. Simms.

2. If you could delete one word and only one from each paragraph of the original passage, which word would it be?

3. From "Adjusting the pince-nez" to "past five years", read the sentences aloud and formulate advice to the writer about sentence making.

4. What kind of person is Mr. Simms shown to be?

5. What are the phrases which characterize him?

6. Is the characterization one which arouses interest? If it does not, is it by reason of Mr. Simms' being in-

trinsically uninteresting or by reason of the way he is presented?

7. Is it possible to write an interesting story in which the main figure is personally uninteresting? Support your answer by evidence drawn from your own reading or writing.

8. Can you call to mind some person you know who is consistently dull? So far as your acquaintance with the person allows, record the evidences of dullness and analyze their probable causes.

9. Write a brief sketch of a dull person, showing that the person is dull but making the sketch interesting.

10. ". . . what is to make an impression on a reader must be repeated and re-repeated, ground into his mind by repetition." Beginning with the phrase, "Mr. Simms did not like to complain", count the repetitions of idea in the rest of the paragraph. Since repetition itself is necessary, what makes these repetitions ineffective?

Mrs. Haines

Mrs. Julia Haines, long and lean and blanket-swathed, sat on a bench outside her son-in-law's ranch-house door. It was the tenth week of her ranch residence, and her fifth day of escape from bed.

Inside the house her daughter Mattie, ten weeks a wife, glanced out anxiously now and then in the intervals of her dishwashing. She had not approved of the expedition out of doors, but she had not known how to prevent it. Mattie was not quite seventeen. For sixteen years and six months of her life she had lived and breathed and had her being in strict obedience to her mother's will. The external reasons for that obedience were gone now, but the habit of it remained.

"An' yet I got to take care of her," the daughter admonished herself. "Whether she likes it or not, I got to. Till she gets good an' strong, anyhow."

She tiptoed to the window and looked out. Mrs. Haines sat crumpled upon her bench, her head thrown back, her sallow eyelids drawn close against the sun.

"Asleep," Mattie diagnosed the attitude with satisfaction and went back to her pans.

"Thinks I'm asleep," the invalid interpreted, listening to the retreating footsteps. So deep within her that the haggard mask of face was undisturbed, she was smiling over the misapprehension. Mattie in the role of caretaker filled her mother with satiric mirth.

"Though it was time she growed up," the listener admitted. "I kep' her back long enough. An' she's got a good man."

1. What is the point of observation from which "Mrs. Haines" is written?

2. What advantage, if any, do you see in the writer's having chosen this point?

3. Rewrite the paragraphs given, leaving out none of the information to the reader now included but allowing yourself entrance into only one of the two minds.

4. What influenced you to choose one mind rather than the other?

5. Does the writer, in this first page of his story, show you which of the two characters is to be the more interesting? What attributes are assigned to her to make her the more interesting?

6. In what phrases does the writer show you the social status of the two persons in his story? Their economic status?

7. Where, if at all, do these opening paragraphs suggest the general idea which is to hold the incidents together?

8. Approximately how much time does this opening page actually show? How much does it account for?

---

1. The beginnings of three stories have been given above. Which one should you least unwillingly continue reading?

2. Does any one of the three repel you? What causes it to be repellent?

3. Of these stories, which comes nearest to making

clear time, place, person, circumstance in its opening
paragraphs?

4. Summarize in a sentence your impression of one of
the characters shown.

5. Character, personified trait, and caricature are all
possible in the presentation of persons in a story. Place
each of the persons shown in these beginnings in its
proper category.

II

A

All round the circle of the hills the dazzling sky pressed down unclouded to the touch of the parched rimrock. Between the hills, the shallow basin lay baked and breathless. Over it the tense air quivered with heat. Within, no bird fluttered, no water purled, no green plant raised its head. Only the desert children, sagebrush and greasewood and long-spined cactus, gray but never dying, lived on there in the drought, sterile and forbidding as the land which gave them birth. Everywhere was silence upon the place, everywhere was immobility.

There are hills, rounded, blunt, burned, squeezed up out of chaos, chrome and vermilion painted, aspiring to the snow line. Between the hills lie high level-looking plains full of intolerable sun glare, or narrow valleys drowned in a blue haze. The hill surface is streaked with ash drift and black, unweathered lava flows. After rains water accumulates in the hollows of small closed valleys, and, evaporating, leaves hard dry levels of pure desertness that get the local name of dry lakes. Where the mountains are steep and the rains heavy, the pool is never quite dry, but dark and bitter, rimmed about with the efflorescence of alkaline deposits. A thin crust of it lies along the marsh over the vegetating area, which has neither beauty nor freshness. In the broad wastes open to the wind the sand drifts in hummocks about the stubby shrubs, and between them the soil shows saline traces. The sculpture of the hills here is more wind than water work, though the quick storms do sometimes scar them past many a year's redeeming. In all the Western desert edges there are essays in miniature at the famed, terrible Grand Canon, to which, if you keep on long enough in this country, you will come at last.

— Mary Austin. *The Land of Little Rain.**

For you fare along, on some narrow roadway, through stony labyrinths; huge rock mountains, heaving over your head, on this hand; and under your feet, on that, the roar of winds and echoes howling on you in an almost preternatural manner. Towering rock barriers rise sky high before you, and behind you, and around you. The roadway is narrow, footing none of the best. Sharp turns there are, where it will behoove you to mind your paces; one false step, and you will need no second; in the gloomy jaws of the abyss you vanish, and the spec-

* Excerpt used by permission of Houghton Mifflin Company, publishers

tral winds howl requiem. Somewhat better are the suspension bridges, made of bamboo and leather, though they swing like seesaws; men are stationed with lassos, to gin you dexterously, and fish you up from the torrent, if you trip there.

— Thomas Carlyle. "Essay on Dr. Francis"

———————

1. So far as you can tell without their context, which, if any, of these three passages come under the derogation of being "fine writing"?

2. What quality preserves from that stigma the one or ones which are not "fine writing"?

3. Choosing what seems to you the worst of the excerpts, analyze its faults.

4. Try improving this same excerpt not by additions but only by elisions. Can it, by cutting only, be made noticeably better?

5. In the second excerpt, the words in the first sentence are forced out of their usual order. Replace them in the usual order. Is the sentence more or less effective?

6. Select three descriptive words (adjectives or adverbs) in each excerpt which seem to you either notably effective or notably ill-chosen.

7. For the ill-chosen descriptive words, supply substitutes.

8. Write a brief description of some scene, natural or man-made, which shall bring the scene before the reader's eyes and yet be under no suspicion of "fine writing."

B

That night the lobo wolves howled too near, and Mesquite sat up feverishly, reaching for a gun. Turner pushed him back, reassuring, but the wolves worried him too, as they sent their long-drawn, mournful howls back and forth across the small camp. The little pack burros scuttled to the ends of their ropes, and Turner's black stallion gave a shrill trumpet of fear.

Mesquite wanted to get up. "Danged lobos," he muttered, resisting Turner's attempt to quiet him. "Part of this cheatin' desert. It don't want me to have the gold I found."

Turner whipped out his .45 and fired three reverberating shots towards the unseen wolves. One lobo yelped in pain, and the grinding crunch of teeth on bones mingled with loud growling as the pack fell on their wounded member without waiting for death.

It may be that you remember Lashes. He appeared on the outlaw horizon of one of our large cities a few years ago, a unique artist of bank robbery. His career was meteoric in both brilliance and duration. He displayed the practiced hand and composure of an old-timer, yet he was unknown even to other members of his profession. He worked alone, rapidly, skillfully, collected his swag and effected a complete disappearance. After a time the town became too warm, and on several occasions he escaped capture only by the narrowest margin. Finally after he had been trailed to what was alleged to be his hideout, he dropped out of sight and was heard of no more.

---

1. In the story from which the first of these excerpts is taken, Turner is nursing Mesquite, who has been bitten by a snake. In paragraph four, Turner builds a fire and thus frightens the wolves away. Why does the writer not have him build it sooner?

2. If you were with Turner, what common-sense advice should you give him about his shooting? Why has not the writer applied this common-sense advice for himself?

3. Which of the verbs in the excerpts are effectively used?

4. Is the first excerpt better or worse written than the second?

5. The second excerpt is taken from a detective story. From what point of observation is it written?

6. Given this point of observation, what destructive deviation from it does the writer allow himself?

7. In a detective story, will it be possible to continue with the present point of observation?

8. Contrast the use of verbs in the second excerpt with the use in the first.

9. Limiting yourself to one, what one word or phrase in the second excerpt should you remove? With what should you replace it?

III

(The quotations and questions given in this section are suggestive only. Any reader can readily increase their number for himself.)

1. *The habit of trusting to general assertions and thus sliding away from exact presentation is one no beginner can afford to form.*

a. Give an illustration of an "exact presentation" of character.

b. Change it to generalized statement by removing specific statements.

c. Characterize the same person first by explanation, second by person's action, third by person's speech, fourth by dialogue between two of the person's acquaintances.

2. *No author can compel a reader to carry in mind a dozen differing details.*

a. "Too much of him every way; pervadingly too much nose of a coarse, wrong shape; and his nose in his mind and his manners; too much smile to be real; too much frown to be false; too many large teeth to be visible at once without suggesting a bite." What prevents this characterization from being a presentation by means of many differing details?

b. Write an exact personal description of some individual you know. Underline the phrases, if any, in this exact description which reveal character.

c. For the same person, find a phrase which at once describes and characterizes him.

3. —*it is wise for the beginner to make sure that his own mind is clear as to the difference between characterizing a figure and assigning to it certain identifying marks.*

a. Name the "identifying marks" for some stock character in fiction with which you are familiar.

b. What additions and subtractions are needed to change these identifying marks into characterization?

4. *Once the story is under way, character directs circumstance. Happenings must stop dead or change their course if character be altered, for the happenings continue to exist only because of the kind of person on whom they act.*

a. Find, within your family or among your friends, some person whose character does direct circumstance.

b. Set down as briefly as you can what the qualities of spirit are which cause the person to direct circumstance.

c. Are they necessarily amiable or noble qualities?

d. If in your first choice they are, find one in which circumstances are directed by some especial flaw of temper possessed by the person.

e. From your reading, select a person who directs circumstances and note the qualities assigned him by the author which cause him to do so.

5. *Any figure shown in fiction as in control of his own responses to happening is thereby made greater than happening, though not impervious to it.*

a. Turning back to the text, find which of the excerpts given in *Time* may be used to illustrate this quotation.

b. Provide an illustration from your reading.

c. Write a scene in which the person is shown meeting unfortunate or destructive happening but remaining in control of his own responses to it.

6. *Surprise alone has no fictional value.*

a. Why has it none?

b. How can fictional value be given it?

c. Does the statement hold true of stories whose surprises are in the use of words, not in incident or character — as, for example, in some of O. Henry's stories?

7. *For a beginner, attempts at objective treatment furnish valuable practice, and this whether stories result from the attempts or not.*

a. Why do they furnish valuable practice?

b. Select from the text one excerpt told from another point of observation and retell it objectively.

8. *Stream of consciousness is a name well chosen.*

a. What justification is given for this statement?

b. Write an account of any three or four minutes of time during a given day as the happenings of those minutes appear in the stream of consciousness of one of the persons concerned.

c. Rewrite the passage beginning "She'd been a fool to go" (p. 106), giving it objective treatment but not reducing the reader's knowledge of the distress of mind of the main figure.

IV

Suggested Reading

(The twenty-four stories listed below are to be found not only in the collected works of their authors but also in so many anthologies that especial statement of their placing seems unnecessary. The comment following each draws attention to a conspicuous but by no means a solitary point of technical excellence.)

BIERCE, AMBROSE. "An Occurrence at Owl Creek Bridge." (point of observation, time)

BUNNER, H. C. "The Love Letters of Smith." (repetitions, character)

CABLE, G. W. "Posson Jone'." (character, point of observation)

COBB, IRVIN. "The Belled Buzzard." (repetitions, implication)

CRANE, STEPHEN. "The Open Boat." (time, point of observation)

GALSWORTHY, JOHN. "The Apple Tree." (point of observation, character)

GIBBON, PERCEVAL. "The Second Class Passenger." (time)

GILMAN, CHARLOTTE PERKINS STETSON. "The Yellow Wall Paper." (repetitions, point of observation)

HALE, EDWARD EVERETT. "The Man Without a Country." (repetitions, time)

HARTE, BRET. "The Outcasts of Poker Flat." (point of observation, character)

HARTE, BRET. "Tennessee's Partner." (point of observation, dialogue)

HAWTHORNE, NATHANIEL. "The Great Stone Face." (time, character)

HAWTHORNE, NATHANIEL. "The Minister's Black Veil." (character)

IRVING, WASHINGTON. "A Legend of Sleepy Hollow." (point of observation, character)

JAMES, HENRY. "The Real Thing." (character, dialogue)

JAMES, HENRY. "The Turn of the Screw." (repetitions, implication)

KIPLING, RUDYARD. "Namgay Doola." (dialogue)

KIPLING, RUDYARD. "The Brushwood Boy." (time, repetitions)

POE, EDGAR ALLAN. "The Murders in the Rue Morgue." (repetitions, dialogue)

STEVENSON, R. L. "A Lodging for the Night." (character, time)

STEVENSON, R. L. "Markheim." (time, implication)

STEVENSON, R. L. "The Sire de Malatroit's Door." (time, repetitions)

"TWAIN, MARK." "The Man Who Corrupted Hadleyburg." (repetitions, dialogue)